When in Germany,
DO AS THE
GERMANS DO

The Clued-In Guide to German Life, Language, and Culture

Hyde Flippo

McGraw-Hill

Chicago   New York   San Francisco   Lisbon   London   Madrid   Mexico City
Milan   New Delhi   San Juan   Seoul   Singapore   Sydney   Toronto

Library of Congress Cataloging-in-Publication Data

Flippo, Hyde.
    When in Germany, do as the Germans do : the clued-in guide to German life,
language, and culture / Hyde Flippo.
        p.   cm. (When in— do as the locals do)
    Includes index.
    ISBN 0-8442-2553-3
    1. Germany—Social life and customs.   2. National characteristics, German.
3. Culture shock—Germany.   4. Etiquette—Germany.   I. Title.   II. Series.

DD61 .F55   2002
306′.0943—dc21   2002070055

McGraw-Hill

A Division of The McGraw·Hill Companies

3 4 5 6 7 8 9 0   LBM/LBM   1 0 9 8 7 6 5 4 3

ISBN 0-8442-2553-3

This book was set in Electra
Printed and bound by Lake Book Manufacturing

Cover design by Nick Panos
Cover photograph copyright © Corbis
Interior design by Jennifer Locke
Illustrations by Fred Dolven
Map by Mapping Specialists

McGraw-Hill books are available at special quantity discounts to use as premiums and
sales promotions, or for use in corporate training programs. For more information, please
write to the Director of Special Sales, Professional Publishing, McGraw-Hill, Two Penn
Plaza, New York, NY 10121-2298. Or contact your local bookstore.

This book is printed on acid-free paper.

Contents

Test Yourself Quizlinks

When in Germany, do you know how to fit in by doing as the Germans do? How sensitive are you to German customs and traditions? And how aware are you of contemporary daily life and typical domestic routines of the German people?

The following multiple-choice questions will test how much you know about all aspects of German culture. There are almost a hundred questions in all, each corresponding to a specific article within the book. To discover the answer and more information about the subject, follow the quizlink to the relevant article. Alternatively, you can check the answers listed at the back of the book.

Do as the Germans Do

1. How should you demonstrate your efficiency at work? ►17
   - (a) always leave work on time
   - (b) always work late
   - (c) work late in an emergency

2. What usually happens on your birthday at work? ►18
   - (a) colleagues play tricks on you
   - (b) you are given a cake and small gifts
   - (c) you are expected to provide cake and champagne

3. Which of the following do you need to pay for? ►31
   - (a) public radio
   - (b) public television
   - (c) grocery bags

4. What is an appropriate topic to begin a business meeting? ►32
   - (a) weather
   - (b) family
   - (c) straight down to business

5. Which of the following should you not address as *du*? ►33
   - (a) a child
   - (b) a group of close friends
   - (c) a pet

6. What is the most correct way to attract the attention of a waitress? ►34
   - (a) "Fräulein!"
   - (b) "Frau!"
   - (c) "Frau" plus her surname

7. What do most German men usually wear to work? ►35
   - (a) jeans
   - (b) a sports coat or blazer
   - (c) a suit

8. What should you not ask directions for if you need to relieve yourself? ►36
   - (a) *das Badezimmer*
   - (b) *die Toilette*
   - (c) *das WC*

9. What should you do on entering a restaurant? ►52
   - (a) wait to be seated
   - (b) ask a food server for a table
   - (c) find a table yourself

TEST YOURSELF QUIZLINKS

10. Where should you go to buy prescription medicine? ➤61
    (a) *Drogerie*   (b) *Apotheke*   (c) *Supermarkt*

11. What should you recycle in the "Yellow Sack"? ➤69
    (a) biodegradable waste   (b) packaging materials   (c) glass

12. What does a *"Kehrwoche"* sign outside your apartment oblige you to do for the week? ➤70
    (a) put out recycling   (b) perform cleaning   (c) deliver papers and
                                                              mail duties

13. What sign should you look for in the event of an emergency in a public building? ➤76
    (a) *"Ausgang"*   (b) *"Einstieg"*   (c) *"Notausgang"*

14. Where should you go to buy health foods? ➤77
    (a) *Evergreen*   (b) *Reformhaus*   (c) *Warenhaus*

Places

1. Link each of these three festivals to its region. ➤20
   (a) *Karneval*   (b) *Fosnat*   (c) *Fastnacht*
   (i) Rhineland   (ii) Bavaria   (iii) Baden

2. What guidebook was the first to use the "Baedeker system" in 1839? ➤54
   (a) Baedeker Rhine   (b) Baedeker Paris   (c) Baedeker Venice

3. What Alpine city boasts the longest ski season in the Alps? ➤58
   (a) Garmisch   (b) Innsbruck   (c) Zermatt

4. Berlin is Germany's center for which of these industries? ➤84
   (a) banking   (b) movies   (c) publishing

5. In which city are Mercedes and Porsche based? ➤108
   (a) Munich   (b) Stuttgart   (c) Wolfsburg

6. Which of these cities does not have a metro system? ➤112
   (a) Dresden   (b) Frankfurt am Main   (c) Stuttgart

People

1. To whom is Germany's oldest literary society dedicated? ➤9
   (a) Goethe   (b) Shakespeare   (c) Dante

2. When did Goethe die? ➤10
   (a) 1726   (b) 1785   (c) 1832

3. What saint gives his or her name to New Year's Eve? ➤24
   (a) Silvester   (b) Magdalena   (c) Elisabeth

4. Who is Udo Lindenberg? ➤46
   (a) a pop star   (b) a soccer star   (c) a late-night television host

5. Who or what is Ötzi? ➤57
   (a) a derogatory term for an East German   (b) an Alpine ice man   (c) a popular clown

6. What was the true profession of the famed impostor called the Captain from Köpenick? ➤62
   (a) librarian   (b) cobbler   (c) chimney sweep

7. As what is Anne-Sophie Mutter famous? ➤63
   (a) film director-actress   (b) Nobel physicist   (c) violinist

8. Which of these German chancellors was not a Socialist? ➤88
   (a) Helmut Schmidt   (b) Helmut Kohl   (c) Willy Brandt

9. Who translated the first Germanic Bible? ➤92
   (a) Ulfilas   (b) Gutenberg   (c) Luther

10. Who designed Berlin's Jewish Museum? ➤93
    (a) Ludwig Mies van der Rohe   (b) Richard Rogers   (c) Daniel Libeskind

11. Who invented aspirin? ➤95
    (a) Friedrich Bayer   (b) Felix Hoffmann   (c) Gustav Aspirin

12. For what is Dr. Magnus Hirschfeld known? ➤106
    (a) founder of Zionism   (b) father of gay rights movement   (c) discovered cure for syphilis

Organizations

1. What is the largest bank in the German-speaking world? ➤14
   (a) Deutsche Bank   (b) UBS   (c) Credit Suisse Group

2. Where is the European Central Bank based? ➤15
   (a) Frankfurt   (b) Stuttgart   (c) Berlin

3. Which of these companies is not owned by a German corporation? ➤16
   (a) RCA Records   (b) MTV   (c) Random House

4. Which of these U.S. retailers has not entered the German market? ➤27
   (a) Lands' End   (b) Wal-Mart   (c) Safeway

5. What company bought up popular German website Ricardo.de? ➤29
   (a) E-bay   (b) Amazon.com   (c) Yahoo

6. What does the German Language Society recognize every year? ➤79
   (a) national dictation   (b) top words   (c) bureaucratic
   winners   doublespeak

7. Members of what organization are barred from government jobs in Bavaria? ➤94
   (a) Communist party   (b) Bündnis 90   (c) Church of
   Scientology

8. Which of these benefits can you expect from the German telecom market? ➤98
   (a) free local calls   (b) flat-rate calls   (c) choice of carrier

9. What is the standard suffix for German websites? ➤100
   (a) .bd   (b) .de   (c) .ge

Time

1. In what period are Karl May's popular novels set? ➤11
   (a) Roman Empire   (b) Crusades   (c) Wild West

2. How are summer vacations in Germany staggered? ➤21
   (a) by profession/industry   (b) by state   (c) by first letter of
   surname

3. What traditional holiday does Halloween precede? ➤22
   (a) *Christi Himmelfahrt*   (b) *Allerheiligen*   (c) *Heilige Drei Könige*

4. At what age must German students decide their type of secondary schooling? ➤41
   (a) 10   (b) 12   (c) 13

5. Approximately when was Berlin founded? ➤56
   (a) 150 B.C.   (b) A.D. 750   (c) A.D. 1200

6. What is celebrated on October 3? ➤64
   (a) the founding of the   (b) German reunification   (c) the collapse of the
   Federal Republic   Berlin Wall

7. What are the normal lengths of mortgages? ➤66
   (a) 5 and 10 years   (b) 10 and 15 years   (c) 15 and 30 years

8. How long must youths serve in the military? ►86
   (a) not compulsory   (b) 10 months   (c) 16 months

9. How long must you live in Germany before being eligible to apply for citizenship? ►102
   (a) 3 years   (b) 8 years   (c) 15 years

10. How long can a non-German drive on a foreign license in Germany? ►110
    (a) 6 months   (b) 9 months   (c) 12 months

Quantity

1. Which of the following is not measured in metric units? ►38
   (a) apartment size   (b) recipe ingredients   (c) tire size

2. Of Germany's 300 universities, how many are private? ►42
   (a) fewer than 5 percent   (b) 5–10 percent   (c) more than 10 percent

3. How many varieties of sausage are there? ►48
   (a) 500   (b) 1,000   (c) 1,500

4. How much mineral water do Germans drink per person per year? ►53
   (a) 47 liters   (b) 71 liters   (c) 101 liters

5. How many inhabitants of Germany are foreigners? ►103
   (a) fewer than 5 percent   (b) 5–10 percent   (c) more than 10 percent

6. How many penalty points result in the loss of a driver's license (drunk driving counts as 7 points)? ►111
   (a) 8 points   (b) 12 points   (c) 18 points

7. How many classes of train travel does Germany offer? ►113
   (a) only one standard class   (b) two   (c) three

Connections

1. What U.S. film was based on Erich Kästner's tale *Das doppelte Lottchen*? ►43
   (a) *Twins*   (b) *The Parent Trap*   (c) *Look Who's Talking*

2. To what U.S. city did the Bauhaus movement transfer? ►12
   (a) Detroit   (b) Philadelphia   (c) Chicago

TEST YOURSELF QUIZLINKS

3. What is the Germanic ancestor of the Punxsutawney Phil groundhog? ➤19
   (a) a beaver   (b) a hedgehog   (c) a porcupine

4. Which of these items can you usefully take to Germany? ➤30
   (a) your ATM card   (b) your mobile phone   (c) your electric alarm clock

5. Which of the following are incompatible between Germany and the United States? ➤44
   (a) CDs   (b) audiocassettes   (c) DVDs

6. How does a typical German washing machine compare with American models? ➤68
   (a) uses more water   (b) spins more slowly   (c) uses hotter water

7. How do German crime figures per capita compare with those of the United States? ➤73
   (a) more burglaries, fewer murders   (b) fewer burglaries, more murders   (c) fewer burglaries, fewer murders

8. How is the word *TV* pronounced in German? ➤78
   (a) TAY-VAY   (b) TEE-VEE   (c) TAY-FOW

9. Which of the following is not a German word? ➤80
   (a) *der Smoking*   (b) *das Lifting*   (c) *der Opening*

What's That?

1. What is BKA? ➤75
   (a) an animal rights terrorist group   (b) summertime hours   (c) the federal police force

2. What is the origin of the *Jugendweihe* celebration? ➤90
   (a) Bavarian Catholicism   (b) North German Lutheranism   (c) East German Communism

3. What is *ein Handy*? ➤97
   (a) a mobile phone   (b) a personal organizer   (c) a recycling bin

4. What are the *oberen Zehntausend* ("upper 10,000")? ➤101
   (a) the upper social elite   (b) the top German businesspeople   (c) the German word used most often

5. What can you pay for with a BahnCard? ➤118
   (a) train tickets   (b) road tolls   (c) parking tickets

Laws and Regulations

1. What are not allowed to open on Sundays? ➤26
   - (a) bakeries
   - (b) gas stations
   - (c) flower shops

2. What is a compulsory feature in the German educational system? ➤40
   - (a) 13 years' education
   - (b) kindergarten
   - (c) religious education

3. What does the *Reinheitsgebot*, the oldest consumer protection law, cover? ➤50
   - (a) bread
   - (b) beer
   - (c) sausage

4. What home appliance is outlawed in Germany? ➤67
   - (a) in-sink garbage disposal
   - (b) leaf blower
   - (c) home brew kit

5. What are German tourists returning from Poland restricted from importing? ➤71
   - (a) cuckoo clocks
   - (b) ceramics
   - (c) garden gnomes

6. What are you not allowed to own without a license? ➤81
   - (a) a radio
   - (b) a dog
   - (c) a computer with an Internet connection

7. What are German film ratings most likely to restrict to "16 and up"? ➤82
   - (a) sexual situation
   - (b) violence
   - (c) strong language

8. What tax is levied on almost all Germans but usually exempts foreign nationals? ➤91
   - (a) national monument tax
   - (b) reconstruction tax
   - (c) church tax

9. What size apartment buildings are required by law to have elevators installed? ➤104
   - (a) two-story and above
   - (b) four-story and above
   - (c) no legal requirement

10. Which of the following is not illegal in Germany? ➤105
    - (a) membership in the Nazi party
    - (b) prostitution
    - (c) mowing your lawn on Sunday

Know What the Germans Know

1. Which tree is most commonly associated with Saint Barbara's Feast (December 4)? ➤23
   - (a) acacia
   - (b) birch
   - (c) cherry

2. What credit card is most widely accepted in Germany? ➤25
   - (a) Visa
   - (b) Eurocard
   - (c) Diner's Card

3. What colors are the new Deutsche Post signs? ➤28
   - (a) red and yellow
   - (b) blue and green
   - (c) black and yellow

TEST YOURSELF QUIZLINKS

4. Which of these grape varieties is a common source of German wines? ➤47
   (a) Shiraz   (b) Sylvaner   (c) zinfandel

5. Which of these treatments is covered by German health insurance? ➤59
   (a) spa visits   (b) liposuction   (c) cosmetic plastic
                                                             surgery

6. Which of these features is most commonly found in German apartments? ➤72
   (a) wall-to-wall carpeting (b) a lock on every   (c) central air-
                                  internal door   conditioning

7. What colors are the uniforms of German police officers? ➤74
   (a) green and brown   (b) black and blue   (c) varies from state to
                                                             state

8. Which publication is the most appropriate to buy for a highbrow colleague? ➤83
   (a) *Bild*   (b) *Stern*   (c) *Die Zeit*

9. Which type of spacecraft took the first German into orbit? ➤96
   (a) Apollo   (b) space shuttle   (c) Soyuz

10. Which is a feature of burial in Germany? ➤107
    (a) no cremation allowed   (b) short-term rights to   (c) recycling of funeral
                                  burial place   caskets

11. What is the fastest train service in Germany? ➤114
    (a) EC   (b) IC   (c) ICE

12. On what type of transportation is a ticket from a *Fahrkartenautomaten* valid? ➤116
    (a) bus   (b) metro and streetcar   (c) all forms

Shakespeare in German: *Der Schwan vom Avon*

Strange as it may seem, the German Shakespeare Society (die Deutsche Shakespeare-Gesellschaft, DSG) is the world's oldest. Founded in 1864, on the occasion of the Bard's 300th birthday (*zum 300. Geburtstag vom Barden*), the society is headquartered in Weimar, a city that is also closely associated with the real "German Shakespeare," Johann Wolfgang von Goethe.

Divided by the Cold War and the Berlin Wall for three decades, Germany's oldest literary society successfully managed its own reunification in 1993. Each year in April, the month of Shakespeare's birth and death, the DSG sponsors its Shakespeare-Tage (Shakespeare Days), an international event that alternates locales between Weimar and Bochum, the former western headquarters. The society also promotes meetings, seminars, and research and publishes a booklike annual journal, *Das Shakespeare-Jahrbuch*, in English and German.

The German fascination with Shakespeare began in the early 1700s when English repertoire companies crossed the Ärmelkanal to perform the Bard's plays all across Germany and Europe. Translations of Shakespeare's words have become so much a part of the German language that Germans can be forgiven if they sometimes seem to forget that William Shakespeare was not Wilhelm Shakespeare. In fact, the Germans take a backseat to no one when it comes to honoring the greatest English poet of all time. They do so by performing and attending his plays (more performances are given each year than in Britain!), using his words and phrases, and joining Shakespeare clubs and associations. There's even a replica of the Globe Theatre in Neuss, not far from Düsseldorf. Each season in Neuss, the German Globe offers a program of Shakespeare productions—in both German and English.

As in the English-speaking world, Germans often fail to realize just how much of their vocabulary comes from Shakespeare. Then again, *was ist ein Name?* (what's in a name?). They would no doubt consider such concerns *viel Lärm um nichts* (much ado about nothing). Worrying about such things could be *der Anfang vom Ende* (the beginning of the end).

Over the years, many German literary figures have translated Shakespeare into the language of Goethe and Schiller. (Among other works, Goethe's "Götz von Berlichingen" shows Shakespeare's influence.) For many of the Bard's plays and sonnets it is possible to find several German versions that have been translated at different times by different poets. Ironically, this means that it is usually easier to read Shakespeare in German (if you're German) than in English! The English of Shakespeare's time is often foreign to modern ears, but the German translations tend to be in more modern German than the Elizabethan English of the originals.

> **Related Web links: shakespeare-gesell schaft.de**—Deutsche Shakespeare-Gesellschaft (German Shakespeare Society) (E, G)

9

Goethe's Bestseller: The Novel That Swept the World in the 1770s

As August 28, 1999, approached, Germany prepared to celebrate the 250th birthday of its best-known cultural icon: Johann Wolfgang von Goethe (1749–1832). It was to be a "*Goethe-Jahr,*" a commemorative year for the German author, poet, dramatist, philosopher, and scientist who continues to hold the undisputed crown as the preeminent symbol of German culture—at home and abroad—more than a century and a half after his death. Although his life and work have been examined, researched, and written about more than that of probably any other German figure in history, the *Goethe-Jahr* inspired even more Goethe frenzy in print, on the air, and on the Web.

Best known for the drama *Faust* and his other classic works of literature, Goethe also dabbled in popular literature. In 1774, he published a novel that became a worldwide bestseller, *Die Leiden des jungen Werthers* (*The Sorrows of Young Werther*). Things moved a little more slowly in those days, and it was three years after the American Revolution before the English translation appeared, in 1779. The first *Sturm und Drang* (storm and stress) novel, *Werther* was written as an exchange of letters between lovers. Its neurotic, egotistical, lovesick teenage central character spawned an 18th-century global rash of rejected-lover suicides similar to that in the novel.

The semiautobiographical *Werther* reflected Goethe's romantic suffering (the more accurate translation of the title's original *Leiden*) over Charlotte Buff in Wetzlar. Goethe even named the love interest in his work Charlotte (Lotte).

No head-in-the-clouds technophobe, Goethe displayed his convictions regarding social and technological progress, most notably in *Wilhelm Meisters Lehrjahre* (*Wilhelm Meister's Travels*), written in 1821–29.

Goethe the Man

Who was this man who provokes such extreme devotion—and criticism—from Germans and others? It's not an easy question to answer.

The "Gothic Shakespeare" was much more than that—a complex figure of numerous contrasts in many fields. In his long life and career (he died only months before his 84th birthday), Goethe the author and poet wrote a worldwide bestselling novel (*Die Leiden des jungen Werthers*, 1774) as well as a landmark of German and world literature—the poetic, deeply philosophical two-part drama *Faust* (Part I, 1808; Part II, 1832). Goethe the scientist and researcher wrote *Metamorphose der Pflanzen* (*The Metamorphosis of Plants*) in 1790 and *Farbenlehre* (*Theory of Color*) in 1805–10. His science might have been faulty (particularly in *Farbenlehre*) and his valid discoveries often made after others, but Goethe's writings on the history of science and his insight into the mental process and the problems of scientific inquiry command respect to this day. And Goethe the philosopher intertwined themes of religion and science in his poetic series titled *Gott und Welt* (*God and World*), published in 1827.

Related Web links: gutenberg.aol.de/autoren /goethe.htm—Projekt Gutenberg, with many of Goethe's works online (G); **dw-world.de**— Deutsche Welle site (E, G)

Cowboys and Indians—Not Necessarily in That Order

The German fascination with *Indianer* and the American Wild West often strikes Americans as odd, but it is a solid element of German culture. Although it is now a fading practice in the age of television and video games, almost every adult in the German-speaking world today read Karl May's tales of the West as a child. You may never have heard of Karl May (pronounced MY), but he is the German Zane Grey or Louis L'Amour (also popular authors in German translation). A series of Western films in the 1960s and '70s based on May's books helped promote the German fascination with the American West.

Karl May was born into poverty near Chemnitz in 1842. Though scorned by the literary establishment, at his death in 1912, May had become one of Germany's best-read authors. His adventure tales of people and places he had never seen became popular fare for Germany's young readers. Volumes 1–33 made up his so-called travel adventures. Among the most popular figures in May's many books were the Indian Winnetou and his paleface friend Old Surehand. (Germans and Europeans have always favored the Indians over the cowboys!) Some of May's works have been translated into other languages, but they are hard to find.

In recent years in Germany, there has been a trend toward counteracting the romantic picture of Native Americans that May's books helped create. One current website asks (in German): "Is your image of Indians still mostly influenced by Winnetou?" Another German site is sponsored by the Native American Association of Germany e.V., which tries to update the German and European view of Indians and publicize related events in Europe, including genuine powwows.

Nevertheless, to this day there are traditional Western and Indian clubs all across Germany, some with their own Wild West saloon and/or Western fort. German summer camps offer *Tipi-Dörfer*, or tepee villages. The popular *Karl-May Festspiele* ("pageants") scattered around Germany still draw visitors who want to be entertained by outdoor re-creations of the stories about Winnetou. The most famous of these pageants, in Bad Segeberg, featured the actress Elke Sommer during the 1999 season (June through August). Two other European stars who used to play Winnetou in the movies, Pierre Brice and Gojko Mitic, were on hand for the production called *"Halbblut"* (Half-Breed), based on Karl May stories. One such pageant announced that attendance for 1999 was above the previous year. It seems the German love of the romantic Indian legend continues.

Related Web links: members.aol.com/adlerpost /start.htm Adlerpost/Eagle Mail—an online German news source for events related to Native Americans, with some English articles (E, G); karlmay.uni-bielefeld.de—Karl-May-Gesellschaft (KM Society, KMG) presents the life and work of the author (G); karlmay.uni-bielefeld.de/kmg/ sprachen/englisch/primlit/index.htm—KMG, some of Karl May's works in English (E); karl-may-museum.de—Karl May Museum, near Dresden (G);

Bauhaus: From Gropius to Jahn

The Bauhaus connection spans over many decades. What links the cities of Dessau and Chicago, and connects the architects Walter Gropius, Ludwig Mies van der Rohe, and Helmut Jahn (the latter born more than half a century after Gropius and Mies van der Rohe)? The Bauhaus is the link.

The "house of building" design movement that originated in Germany around the beginning of the 1920s continues to exert an enormous influence on international architecture and design. Although the Bauhaus and its influences have as many detractors as proponents, there is no denying the movement's significant impact on structures as diverse as skyscrapers and teapots.

The Bauhaus (1919–33) is inseparable from its founder, German architect Walter Gropius (1883–1969). The famous school of art and industrial design (architecture was not officially added until 1927) was first established in Weimar. Officially known as the Staatliches Bauhaus Weimar, the school remained there until local resistance and financial difficulties forced a move to Dessau in 1925. Soon the Bauhaus had attracted an impressive cadre of artists and architects, including Paul Klee, Wassily Kandinsky, Lyonel Feininger, and Ludwig Mies van der Rohe.

Gropius (along with several other soon-to-be famous architects) worked for a time in the Berlin offices of German architect Peter Behrens (1868–1940) and was greatly influenced by him, particularly while working on Behrens's projects for the huge German electrical concern AEG.

As with most other things German, the Bauhaus also has its connection with the "German past" and the Nazis. With the advent of the Hitler regime, Gropius and his "decadent" school of design became unwelcome anywhere in Germany. After a brief move to Berlin, the Bauhaus was shut down in 1933. The "New Bauhaus" (later the Institute of Design) was reestablished in the New World in Chicago by the artist Laszlo Maholy-Nagy in 1937. At the same time, Gropius went to Harvard University and was soon appointed chair of the School of Architecture. He became a U.S. citizen in 1944 and remained at Harvard until his retirement in 1952. Gropius was active in The Architects Collaborative design firm, founded in 1946, until his death in 1969.

In 1938, Bauhaus protégé Mies van der Rohe (1886–1969) became the head of what was later known as the Illinois Institute of Technology (IIT) in Chicago and designed its brand-new campus. Almost three decades later, in 1966, Helmut Jahn (born in 1940) began his graduate studies in architecture at IIT. In 1981, Jahn became a principal in the Chicago architectural firm of Murphy/Jahn. That same year, Jahn, like Gropius before him, became a professor of architecture at Harvard. Today the Nuremberg-born Jahn is a renowned international architect working on projects in Germany, the United States, and all over the world.

Related Web links: bauhaus.de—Bauhaus-Archiv, Berlin, a good site with biographies of all the main figures (G); **craton.geol.brocku.ca/ guest/jurgen/bauhaus.htm**—one of the best Bauhaus sites, by a geologist! (E); **iit.edu**— Illinois Institute of Technology, see College of Architecture (E); **archinform.de/arch/277.htm**— Helmut Jahn Projects (E, G); **skyscrapers.com/ deutsch/worldmap/city**—skyscrapers in Frankfurt am Main ("Mainhattan") (E, G)

The roof of the Sony Center on Berlin's Potsdamer Platz

Banks and *Sparkassen*

Banking in the German-speaking world has a long tradition going back to the 14th century and the banklike dealings of the north German Hanseatic League (*Hansa*). In the 15th and 16th centuries, the Augsburg-based Fugger money-lending and commercial dynasty held kings and emperors (kaisers) in its debt. Later, the House of Rothschild, based in Frankfurt am Main, carried on the far-reaching German banking tradition in the 19th century.

For travelers and those planning to live and work in German Europe today, the first word to learn is *Geldautomat*, German for *ATM*. While not long ago, the German-speaking countries lagged behind the rest of Europe in ATMs per customer, today even Germans have discovered the obvious convenience of *Geldautomaten*—which means that you will have little difficulty finding one nearby, even in smaller, out-of-the-way locations. Germany's *Sparkassen* (savings banks) alone have more than 14,000 ATMs scattered across the land. At last count, there were 11,427 *Geldautomaten* in Germany displaying the "Plus" logo. As long as you remember your personal identification number (PIN, *Geheimzahl*), you'll have easy access to cash by using your debit or credit card in Austria, Germany, or Switzerland. Besides the convenience, the ATM exchange rate and any fees are usually more favorable to you than those for traveler's checks.

German banks can be divided roughly into five categories:

1. large commercial banks
2. government-owned state and regional wholesale banks
3. savings banks (*Sparkassen*)
4. the smaller but ubiquitous cooperative credit banks (*Raiffeisenbanken, Volksbanken*)
5. the recently privatized postal savings bank system (Postbank AG)

Austria and Switzerland have similar systems, including postal savings banks.

German (D) and Swiss (CH) Banks in the World Top 25 (with world rank)

1. Deutsche Bank D (3)
2. HypoVereinsbank D (7)
3. UBS CH (8)
4. Credit Suisse Group (11)
5. Dresdner Bank D (16)
6. Commerzbank D (20)
7. Landesbank Baden-Württemberg D (39)
8. DG Bank D (41)
9. Kreditanstalt für Wiederaufbau D (47)
10. Bankgesellschaft Berlin D (48)

Rankings are for 2000. Source: *Banker's Almanac*, November 1, 2000

Related Web links: german-banks.com—German Association of Banks (BdB) (E, G); bank24.de—Bank 24 (G); http://group .deutsche-bank.de—Deutsche Bank (G); ubs.ch—UBS Bank, Switzerland (E, G); snet.de—Sparkassen im Internet (G); mastercard.com—see *ATM Locator* (E)

€ for Euro: Germany Says "auf Wiedersehen" to the Mark

The 2002 arrival of euro (€) coins and bills made Germans nervous. Even though the European Central Bank, the clearinghouse for the new European currency, is located in Frankfurt (a city so dotted with bank skyscrapers, its nickname is "Bankfurt"), the euro had been little more than an abstract concept since its birth as a cashless currency in eleven countries on January 1, 1999. In a nation that experienced hyperinflation and worthless money in the 1920s, the collapse of the **Reichsmark** after World War II, and the rise of the rocksolid **Deutsche Mark** (DM), the untested euro was just another cause of German angst. Although former German chancellor Helmut Kohl and his government were enthusiastic backers of both the European Union and the euro, average Germans never displayed much enthusiasm for Europe's answer to the U.S. dollar.

Despite the average German's support for the idea of European unity, trading marks for euros was a much harder sell. A 1998 poll conducted six months before the (cashless) euro was first introduced indicated that almost two-thirds of Germans had reservations about the loss of their familiar marks. A legal challenge to the euro by four German university professors was rejected by the country's highest court in April 1998.

Neighboring Austrians were also reluctant to adopt the euro, but at least they could take comfort in the fact that the colorful new euro banknotes were designed by Robert Kalina of the Austrian National Bank. (The winning design for the euro coins came from a Belgian.) The dozen euro zone countries (Greece was added in 2000) from Finland to Portugal and Ireland to Austria first had actual euro money in hand in January 2002. Proponents of the new universal European money see it encouraging more cross-border trade and easier price comparisons among the various euro countries. Euro detractors see it as one more step toward a homogenized Europe lacking any individuality.

Travel in the euro zone certainly has been made easier. Tourists or businesspeople crossing the Austrian-German border no longer have to worry about the exchange rate between the **Deutsche Mark** and the Austrian **Schilling**, since prices on both sides of the border are now in euros. Old marks and schillings, along with francs, lire, pesetas, and so forth, can now be exchanged for euros only at banks. The euro is also very much intended as an alternative to the domination of the U.S. dollar as a world currency and, unlike the dollar, offers notes in denominations over 100. The 500-euro bill may prove a popular replacement for the ubiquitous 100-dollar bill.

Related Web links: ihr-euro.de—German euro website (G); **http://euro.eu.int**—the EU's euro site (E, G)

The Germans Are Coming: A German Economic Invasion?

Many German corporations and products are household names all over the world. Few people would fail to recognize brands such as Adidas, Bayer, BMW, Lufthansa, Mercedes, or Volkswagen. However, the November 1998 merger of Daimler-Benz and Chrysler not only made news around the world but also brought home a recent trend: German companies buying up U.S. companies. German corporations and banks seem to be expanding globally, chiefly by taking over or merging with American firms. Deutsche Bank bought New York–based Bankers Trust. Bertelsmann purchased Random House. (Bertelsmann already owned half of Barnes & Noble and shares of other U.S. companies, including America Online.)

DaimlerChrysler AG, the historic union of Germany's Daimler-Benz AG and America's 73-year-old Chrysler Corporation, became the world's third largest automaker, measured by financial size, just behind General Motors and Ford Motor Company. The company incorporates the Chrysler, Dodge, Plymouth, and Jeep vehicles made by the old Chrysler Corporation, with Mercedes-Benz cars and Freightliner trucks made by the former Daimler-Benz AG. The new Daimler-Chrysler has headquarters in Stuttgart and Auburn Hills, Michigan, near Detroit. Former Chrysler shareholders now control 42 percent of DaimlerChrysler, with former Daimler-Benz holders making up a majority 58 percent.

Daimler-Benz may be a familiar name, but how many Americans have ever heard of Bertelsmann? This closely held company, owned by the Mohn family of Germany, exerts influence far beyond its name recognition. In addition to Bertelsmann's recent U.S. acquisitions, the media giant, headquartered in the small town of Gütersloh, owns or controls the American publishers Bantam DoubledayDell as well as RCA Records and BMG Music.

But Americans don't need to worry—and they don't seem to be doing so. American investment overseas is still more than 25 percent greater than total foreign investment in the United States. And the U.S. economy is still the largest in the world, with Japan ranking second and Germany third. Of the top 20 companies in the world at the end of 1998, 15 were American. The rest were Japanese (2), Anglo-Dutch (1), British (1), or Swiss (1).

Recently, a well-known brand name in Germany was sold to a British firm. In 1998, America's Woolworth Corporation sold off its last remaining five-and-dime stores in Germany. Known as "Woolworth" in Germany, the retail chain had been a familiar "German" name. Back in 1890, F. W. Woolworth himself visited Germany. Soon after, Woolworth stores in the United States were selling glass Christmas decorations from the small German town of Lauscha (Thuringia).

> **Related Web links: adidas.de**—Adidas (E, G); **aol.de**—AOL Germany (G); **bmg.com**—BMG Music is a Bertelsmann company (E); **daimlerchrysler.com**—DaimlerChrysler (G, E); **http://german-way.com**—business links for Austria, Germany, and Switzerland (E, G)

German Efficiency: Order Is a German Virtue

"*Ordnung muss sein,*" or "There must be order," is a universal German saying. But there is order, and there is order. Germans believe in order but only until it's time to get in line, or queue up. Then order can go to the dogs! At the bank or bus stop, it's chaos and every man and elbow for himself. Not very efficient.

While German homes display an utterly amazing tidiness, with everything in its place and ready for a white-glove inspection at any minute, in the workplace this obsession with order and compartmentalization can, however, promote inefficiency by hindering communication and impeding the sharing of information. Though open work spaces and an "open-door policy" have been implemented by some German firms, they are still the exception.

Germans are good at talking about and describing efficiency, but when it comes to actual implementation, things frequently fall apart. Take the train system. You used to be able to set your watch by the departure of trains run by the former Deutsche Bundesbahn, the old German Federal Railway. But ever since the 1994 privatization of the former east and west German railroads that created the new Deutsche Bahn AG (DB), Germans have taken to saying that the only thing the DB schedule tells you is when your train *won't* arrive or depart. In addition, a series of recent rail breakdowns and disasters, the most serious being the 1998 crash of a high-speed ICE train in Eschede that killed 98 people, has further derailed DB's reputation for safety and efficiency.

Perhaps the worst recent example of German inefficiency is the banking crisis in the city and state of Berlin. Berlin's government-owned banks had to be bailed out of bankruptcy to the tune of 4 million euros!

On the other hand, if you want to see German efficiency at its best, just be in an office at quitting time. It is considered a sign of inefficiency to work overtime. Precisely at quitting time (*Feierabend*), they're out of there! After all, *Pünktlichkeit* (punctuality) is also a German virtue.

Related Web link: emergency.com/grmtrain .htm—Disaster Operations Archive on Eschede rail crash (E)

Happy Birthday? *Alles Gute zum Geburtstag*!

If you thought that birthdays are celebrated pretty much the same all over the world, you'd be wrong. One of the best examples of a custom being turned upside down is the way German speakers celebrate birthdays. When you find out how this works, you may want to keep your own *Geburtstag* a top secret.

In sharp contrast to the procedure in English-speaking countries, the birthday boy or girl (*Geburtstagskind*) in Austria, Germany, or Switzerland is expected to put on the party, provide the cake, and pay for the drinks! It is the one having the birthday who treats friends and family to the celebration, not the other way around.

It is not unusual for German parents to give their son or daughter 50 euros or more to help finance a birthday bash for friends at a local restaurant. The poor birthday boy or girl often spends most of the days leading up to the party slaving over preparations, sometimes even baking the cake and working on the party decorations.

Adults at work are expected to offer cake or some other treat to coworkers. Usually a glass of champagne (*Sekt*) or other bubbly refreshment is also expected by fellow employees. And the older you are, the bigger the birthday bash is expected to be. If word leaks out that someone has a birthday, a crowd of friends and acquaintances (some the birthday person may never have seen before!) will soon gather for the customary treats.

Horoskop: **What's your sign (*Zeichen*)?**

The German *Tierkreiszeichen* (signs of the zodiac) reflect the animal or person associated with each sign: *Stier* (Taurus) is the bull, *Zwillinge* (Gemini) is the twins, and so forth.

In the following list, dates are shown in German format (e.g., 22.12–19.1 means December 22–January 19).

Steinbock (Capricorn): 22.12–19.1
Wassermann (Aquarius): 20.1–18.2
Fische (Pisces): 19.2–20.3
Widder (Aries): 21.3–20.4
Stier (Taurus): 21.4–20.5
Zwillinge (Gemini): 21.5–20.6
Krebs (Cancer): 21.6–22.7
Löwe (Leo): 23.7–22.8
Jungfrau (Virgo): 23.8–22.9
Waage (Libra): 23.9–22.10
Skorpion (Scorpio): 23.10–21.11
Schütze (Sagittarius): 22.11–21.12

Related Web links: online-grusskarten.de—online greeting cards (G); **german.about .com/library/blzod_intro.htm**—the zodiac in German (E)

Groundhog Day: *Mariä Lichtmess*/Candlemas

February 2, *Mariä Lichtmess*—or Candlemas—was an official holiday in Germany until 1912. The day has also been known as *Mariä Reinigung, das Fest der Darstellung des Herrn,* and *Mariä Kerzenweihe.* The latter name (*Kerze* means "candle") is related to the English "Candlemas," with its tradition of blessing both sacred and household candles on February 2.

The American observance of Groundhog Day has its roots in this February holiday. At least as early as the 1840s, German immigrants in Pennsylvania had introduced the tradition of weather prediction that was associated with the hedgehog (*Igel*) in their homeland. Since there were no hedgehogs in the region, the Pennsylvania Germans adopted the indigenous woodchuck (a name derived from an Algonquian word), also known as the groundhog. The town of Punxsutawney has played up the custom over the years and managed to turn itself into the center of the annual Groundhog Day, particularly after the 1993 movie starring Bill Murray and Andie MacDowell. Every year on February 2, people gather to wait to see whether a groundhog known as "Punxsutawney Phil" will see his shadow after he emerges from his burrow. If he does, the tradition says that there will be six more weeks of winter. (Unfortunately, Phil has a rather disappointing 39 percent rate of accuracy for his predictions.)

A similar German legend is connected with Saint Swithin's Day (*Siebenschläfer,* June 27), for which tradition says that if it rains on that day, it will rain for the next seven weeks. But the *Siebenschläfer* is a dormouse, not a hedgehog.

Related Web link: groundhog.org—the Official Punxsutawney Groundhog Club, for origins of the tradition, see History (E)

Die Fünfte Jahreszeit: The Fifth Season

Germans call the pre-Lenten carnival season *die närrische Saison* (the foolish season) or *die fünfte Jahreszeit* (the fifth season). Except for Munich's Oktoberfest, it is the one time of year when many normally staid Germans (and Austrians and Swiss) loosen up and go a little crazy. *Fastnacht*, or *Karneval*, is a "movable feast" (*ein beweglicher Festtag*) that depends on the date of Easter (*Ostern*). In 2002, *Fastnacht* fell on February 12. The official start of the *Fasching* season is either January 7 (the day after Epiphany, *Dreikönige*) or the 11th day of the 11th month (*Elfter im Elften*, November 11), depending on the region. That gives the carnival guilds (*Zünfte*) three to four months to organize each year's events (balls, parades, royalty) leading up to the big bash the week before Ash Wednesday (*Aschermittwoch*), when the Lenten season (*die Fastenzeit*) begins.

Carnival in Rio is probably the world's most famous. In the United States, New Orleans is well known for Mardi Gras. While it is one of a few cities in the United States with a carnival celebration, close to all of the Catholic regions and cities across the German-speaking world, as well as the rest of Europe celebrate Mardi Gras in a big way. Only a few Protestant areas in northern and eastern Germany also observe *Karneval*. Some of Germany's best-known celebrations are held in Cologne, Mainz, Munich, and Rottweil. Germanic carnival celebrations vary from region to region, sometimes even taking place at different times. (The *Fasnacht* event in Basel, Switzerland, happens a week after most other carnivals.)

Carnival, or Mardi Gras, goes by many names in German, depending on the region and dialect—*Karneval* (Rhineland), *Fasching* (Austria, Bavaria), *Fastnacht* (Baden, Switzerland), *Fosnat* (Franconia), or *Fasnet* (Swabia). Whether it's *Fasching* or *Karneval*, it's a time to let off steam and live it up before the Lenten period that once called for fasting (*die Fastenzeit*). It is this fasting tradition that gave the celebration its *Fastnacht* name (night before fasting). In the 15th and 16th centuries, amusing plays known as *Fastnachtspiele* were performed during the pre-Lenten season. Today there are elaborate parades (*Umzüge*) in all the large and small communities where *Fasching* is celebrated. Floats and marchers displaying large caricature heads often lampoon regional and national politicians. Another part of the celebration involves carnival royalty (princes, princesses) and a sort of "countergovernment" during the season. The Rhineland *Rosenmontagumzug* is an event broadcast each year on German television, much like the Macy's Thanksgiving parade in New York.

Fastnacht/Karneval

The word *Fastnacht* is related to the Germanic word *fasten* (to fast; abstain from eating). *Karneval* is related to the Latin *carnem levare* (to remove meat).

Related Web links: karneval.de—Cologne Karneval (E, G); **mainzer-fastnacht.de**—Mainz Fastnacht (G); **infotech.tu-chemnitz.de/~hsc /karneval/worldwide/worldwide.html**—German and world carnival sites (G)

Summer Vacation and *Reisewellen*: Germany's Summer Brings a Wave of Traffic Jams (*Staus*)

The Germans have a word for it: *Sommerferienregelung*. This very logical and reasonable German practice of "summer vacation regulation" staggers the start of the annual summer vacation season among each of the country's 16 states (*Bundesländer*) and is supposed to avoid the chaos that would ensue if all 16 states ended school for the summer on the same day. In theory, at least, *Sommerferienregelung* means that all 82 million Germans don't hit the road on the same day as they head out for their sacred summer vacation in Austria, Italy, Scandinavia, or elsewhere. A national schedule for this and other school holidays is drawn up years in advance. In 2001, for instance, the students of Hessen were the first to leave their books behind for the summer (on June 21), while farther to the south in Bavaria and Baden-Württemberg, *Schüler* and *Studenten* weren't free until more than a month later (on July 26). During the intervening weeks, students in Germany's 13 other states were released on similarly staggered dates. On average, all of the students have about five weeks of freedom before they have to return to the classroom in August or September.

In reality, despite the staggered vacation starts, Germany's highways and autobahns are no place for people with claustrophobia, as each wave of summer vacationers (*Reisewelle*) creates a series of *Staus*, or traffic jams, that can spread out for miles and miles (or kilometers and kilometers). Although there are no longer any border formalities on the German-Austrian border, traffic tends to clog up on many popular routes, including the Brenner Pass autobahn and stretches around and between Salzburg and Vienna.

Related Web link: uni-jena.de/~zep/ferien
.html—*Sommerferienregelung bis 2002* (German summer vacation schedules to 2002) (G)

So-called "beach baskets" (Strandkörbe) await rental at a German Baltic beach.

It's Halloween: *Streich oder Süßigkeit*!

Halloween isn't really a German holiday. There is no actual German equivalent of "Trick or treat" (roughly, *Streich oder Süßigkeit*). It has only been in the last few years that Halloween has been celebrated in Austria and Germany at all, and the holiday is observed mostly in the form of Halloween-themed parties.

Not that Halloween doesn't fit in with other German celebrations, particularly the carnival season of masks and costumes observed in Catholic regions. But the traditional *Allerheiligen* (All Saints' Day, November 1) observation has recently been spiced up with pumpkins, ghosts, and costumes. Suddenly, the uniquely American holiday has become an October phenomenon in Austria and Germany.

Of course, the All Hallows' Eve celebration wasn't originally American either. Halloween, which began as a Celtic/Anglo-Saxon celebration of the end of summer and the start of the Celtic year, was imported to North America by Irish immigrants in the late 1800s. In recent years, no doubt with some help from Hollywood and television, Halloween has jumped from America to German Europe.

Today German newspapers carry stories about the rise in sightings of Halloween decorations and lighted pumpkins in German cities. Articles describe how to make a jack-o'-lantern, and the demand for pumpkins in the fall is growing

The Austrian town of Retz, not far from Vienna, holds an annual Halloween festival, complete with pumpkins and a *Halloween-Umzug* (Halloween pageant), and the region around Retz has become known for its annual pumpkin harvest. Each year, Halloween parties seem to become more prevalent—among adults, teens, as well as youngsters. More and more German department stores carry Halloween-related items in October. Hamburg's House of Horror specialty store, which opened for business in 1996, does an increasingly brisk business for Halloween. Some observers even see Halloween becoming a major retail factor in Germany, perhaps approaching the number two position (after Christmas) that the holiday holds in the United States.

Related Web link: geisterparty.com—Halloween & *Geisterparty*, for party ideas (G)

Barbarazweig—Saint Barbara's Branch

The patron saint of miners, artillerymen, and firefighters, *die heilige Barbara* (Saint Barbara, d. 306) has lent her name to a Germanic Christmas custom that has its roots (literally) in the pre-Christian era. The legend of her martyrdom, on the other hand, seems to have originated around the seventh century. Officially, she is one of the 14 auxiliary saints, or holy helpers.

December 4 is the feast day of Saint Barbara, and this date plays a key role in the custom that bears the name of this virgin martyr. According to legend, Barbara lived in Asia Minor in what is today Turkey. Her father was the pagan emperor Dioscorus, a suspicious, untrusting fellow who persecuted Christians and kept his daughter a virgin by locking her up in a tower whenever he was away.

One day when he returned home, Dioscorus noticed that the tower where he kept his daughter under lock and key now had three windows instead of two. Puzzled, he asked her why she had added a window in his absence. Barbara then made the mistake of confessing that she had become a Christian and the three windows represented the trinity of her new faith. Incensed, her father demanded that she renounce this heresy. After some time had passed and she still stubbornly refused to deny her new religion, he commanded that she be tortured and beheaded. The legend further says that immediately following this gruesome event, Dioscorus was struck dead by lightning, which may explain why Saint Barbara is often invoked during thunderstorms.

Another important element of the *Barbara-Legende* concerns her imprisonment, which led (according to legend) to the Christmas custom that bears her name. Depressed and alone in her cell, Barbara found a dried cherry tree branch, which she moistened daily with a few drops from her drinking water. She was greatly consoled by the beautiful cherry blossoms that appeared just days before her impending execution.

The Barbara Branch Custom

Traditionally in the German-speaking countries, particularly in Austria and the Catholic regions of Germany, a small cherry branch is cut on December 4, *Barbaratag* (Saint Barbara's Day). Sometimes a twig from another flowering plant or tree—apple, forsythia, plum, lilac, or similar blossoms—may be used, but the cherry tree is most customary and authentic.

The cherry branch (*Kirschzweig*) or other cutting is then placed in water and kept in a warm room. If all goes well, on Christmas Day the twig will display blossoms. If it blooms precisely on December 25, this is regarded as a particularly good sign for the future.

Silvester—New Year's Eve

Of all the German New Year's customs, surely "Dinner for One" has to be the oddest. For more than two decades, not a single New Year's Eve has gone by without this 15-minute English-language television sketch being broadcast all across Germany. A German New Year's Eve just doesn't seem right without hearing the lines known to almost any living German: "'Same procedure as last year, Madam?' 'Same procedure as every year, James.'"

The dialogue is from a comedy sketch filmed in Hamburg in glorious black-and-white in 1963. "Dinner for One, or the 90th Birthday" has become such a perennial staple on German television that at least one German airline even shows it on flights just before and after New Year's Day. Traditionally, Germans gather in front of their televisions every New Year's Eve (*Silvester*) to watch Miss Sophie and her butler, James, become increasingly tipsy.

Why is December 31 called *Silvester* in German? We don't know when Saint Sylvester—or Sankt Silvester—was born, but he was pope (*Papst*) from 314 until he died in Rome on December 31, 335. Legend says that Pope Sylvester cured Roman emperor Constantine I of leprosy (*Aussatz*)—after converting him to Christianity, of course. For this, the grateful emperor supposedly granted the pope the so-called Donation of Constantine, giving him extensive rights to land and power. (This gift now seems to be a forgery going back to the eighth century.)

However, New Year's Day has not always been January 1—even on the Christian calendar. In the early Middle Ages, most of Christian Europe celebrated the beginning of each new year on March 25 (Annunciation Day). The Anglo-Saxons started the new year on March 1 until William the Conqueror made January 1 New Year's Day. (England later returned to the March 25 date.) Although the Julian calendar of Rome had set January 1 as the start of the year, it was not until 1582, with the introduction of the Gregorian calendar, that most of Europe adopted the practice of beginning the year on the first day of January. Pope Gregory had the assistance of the German Jesuit mathematician Christopher Clavius (1537–1612) in refining his new calendar, but the Gregorian calendar was not adopted in German Protestant regions until 1700—and even later in many parts of the world, such as Britain (1751) and Russia (1918).

Einen Guten Rutsch!

Most German speakers are unaware that the traditional New Year's expression *einen guten Rutsch* has nothing to do with "sliding" (*rutschen*) into the New Year. It actually comes from the Hebrew word *rosh*, meaning "head" or "beginning"—thus, the beginning of a new year. Apparently, the expression came into German via the Yiddish expression for "a good beginning"—as in Rosh Hashanah, the Jewish New Year. That makes it just one of many German (and English) expressions that derive from Yiddish.

Related Web link: silvester-online.de—links to hotels and parties for New Year celebrations (G)

Credit and Debit Cards

Schuld is a bad word! In most of Europe, particularly in Britain, France, and Scandinavia, you don't have to think twice about credit card acceptance. In Germany, you do.

Never assume that the nice German restaurant in which you just dined will accept plastic payment. Gas stations (*Tankstellen*) are usually OK, often offering card payment at the pump, and ATMs (*Geldautomaten*) are plentiful and easy to use. But does that multilevel bookstore with all those expensive books take Visa or Master-Card? Better ask. When you're checking in at your hotel, especially a smaller one, look for those familiar credit card logos. Although most of the larger German hotels accept credit cards, many smaller hotels and pensions do not.

After all, this is a country whose national railway, Deutsche Bahn, did not accept credit cards to purchase of train tickets until 1992. Not even travel agents would accept them for DB tickets, while in France you could buy a ticket with plastic at even the remotest train station.

Although the German credit card situation has improved slightly in the last few years, you still can't be sure your card (accepted everywhere else in Europe) will be accepted for a purchase in many stores, even in some very large ones. If you are a European resident and have an EC card, a common type of bank debit card, you can use it like a check or a debit card. But if you're a tourist or a visitor without a European bank account, neither your credit cards nor a hometown bank card may be of any use in some German stores. Many shops that accept the EC card will not accept credit cards. While a German tourist in North America and most other parts of the world can and does use a credit card just about anywhere, the reverse is just not the case.

So, what is behind this Teutonic angst about credit cards? For one thing, a German "credit" card is more like a debit card, usually requiring full payment of the balance each month—and the payment is done automatically by the bank! In addition, shop owners don't like paying the transaction fees (5 percent) for credit cards.

The German aversion to credit in general also may well have something to do with the German language. In German, the word for both "debt" and "guilt" is the same: *Schuld*.

Credit Card Acceptance

A comparison of France (population 58 million) and Germany (population 82 million) reveals a big difference in the rate of credit card acceptance by stores and businesses in each country. Despite Germany's much greater population, the country has 250,000 fewer locations that accept MasterCard than in neighboring France. That's all the more surprising when one is aware that Visa is more widely used in France than Eurocard/MasterCard—and vice versa in Germany.

Related Web links: europay.com—Europay International (E); eurocard.de—Eurocard Germany, MasterCard in Europe (G); visa.com—Visa International (E)

Shopping and *das Ladenschlussgesetz*

"We came, we saw, we did a little shopping." Contrary to that bit of graffito from the late Berlin Wall, Germany has never been especially kind to shoppers. Compared with most of the rest of Europe, the German-speaking countries have had a tradition of limited shopping hours and an attitude on the part of salespeople that turned the phrase *customer service* into an oxymoron.

Germany's strict store-closing law, *das Ladenschlussgesetz*, dates back to 1956. Since then, ostensibly to protect the German family and workers, the country's unions and shopkeepers have conspired to maintain hours that favor store owners and employees over the customer.

That situation began to change in the 1990s, when Germans fed up with stores that were always closed when they got off work exerted pressure on their legislators to recognize the modern times. Many German families today have two breadwinners, with neither free to shop during the traditional shopping hours of 8:00 A.M. to 6:30 P.M. on weekdays and 8:00 A.M. to 2:00 P.M. on Saturdays (until 4:00 P.M. once a month). An exception allowed bakeries to open a little earlier—Germans do like their fresh bread! But on Sundays, there is still a virtual shopping blackout. Except for tourist areas, restaurants, and gas stations (and their minimarts), "Never on Sunday" takes on a whole new meaning.

The first small opening in the shopping-hours door came in 1989 with the addition of Thursday late shopping. Even though stores were then permitted to remain open until 8:30 P.M., many smaller shops continued to close at 6:00 or 6:30 P.M. on Thursday. Even today, many smaller shops and some banks still close for "siesta" between noon and 2:00 P.M. The shopping-hours debate crossed a notable landmark in 1993 when a court decision established the right of shops in airports and train stations, as well as the popular gas station minimarts, to sell "travel necessities" even to nontravelers after hours.

In 1996, the most dramatic change in Germany's *Ladenschlussgesetz* occurred. Just before the Christmas shopping season that year, German lawmakers granted retail businesses the right to remain open from 6:00 A.M. to 8:00 P.M. every weekday and until 4:00 P.M. on Saturdays. Bakeries were finally allowed to sell fresh rolls on Sunday—but only for two hours.

In late summer 1999, the German shopping debate increased in intensity when stores in Berlin, Leipzig, and Halle in the German East attempted to bend the closing law and open for Sunday shopping. Legal challenges ended their attempt, but the ongoing debate split Germans into those who want to have more shopping freedom and less regulation, and those who consider Sunday shopping one more step toward shopping chaos and the ruination of the German family.

There's a good reason why the eastern states have taken the lead in the German shopping-hours debate: Communist East Germany had more liberal store hours than its western capitalistic neighbor. In the GDR, shoppers had less to buy, but they had more time to buy it.

Lands' End and Wal-Mart Versus German Law

Nothing better illustrates the differences between the German and American styles of doing business than the hurdles that U.S. retailers such as Lands' End and Wal-Mart have encountered in entering the German market.

Based in Mettlach, Germany, Lands' End GmbH, a division of the U.S. mail-order clothing company, ran up against Germany's so-called Law Against Unfair Competition (*Gesetz gegen den unlauteren Wettbewerb*) when it attempted to advertise its standard refund policy. The German agency that enforces the unfair-competition law wanted to prevent Lands' End from advertising its policy of refunding a dissatisfied customer's money at any time for any reason. Lands' End appealed the decision. Using some bizarre logic, Germany's high court ruled that Lands' End was free to honor its refund policy but that advertising it was verboten as unfair competition.

Wal-Mart Stores, Inc., first entered German retailing in 1997 when it purchased 21 "hypermarket" stores from Germany's Wertkauf AG. Since then, Wal-Mart has expanded its European holdings by buying more German superstores from SPAR Handels AG and the British ASDA supermarket chain. In the process, Wal-Mart has shaken some of German retailing's basic foundations and made a lot of people very nervous, including competitors, trade unions, and regulators.

Like Lands' End, Wal-Mart has been sued because of one of its long-standing policies. For years, the "Everyday Low Prices" retailer has promised to match competitors' prices. A German watchdog group sued Wal-Mart, claiming that its policy must apply to all customers, not just those who call a price difference to Wal-Mart's attention.

Despite such roadblocks, the American retailer seems to be having a noticeable impact on the German market and its competitors. One of Wal-Mart's direct German counterparts, Metro AG, Germany's largest retailer, began to imitate some of Wal-Mart's practices. Metro executives were even seen scoping out the competition in Wal-Mart stores. It wasn't long before Metro's Real-branded hypermarket stores had incorporated Wal-Mart's trademark colors (blue, white, and yellow) into Real's red logo and began opening earlier to match Wal-Mart's 7:00 A.M. early-bird start, and now they even use German-language copies of Wal-Mart's "Everyday Low Prices" slogan. Real has gone so far as to institute a policy that was previously unheard of in Germany: encouraging better customer service by rewarding shoppers with 2.50 euros if they have to wait more than five minutes in a checkout line. German shoppers, accustomed to indifferent and even hostile salesclerks, have been taking notice, and most of the credit goes to an American invader with only 95 stores in Germany.

Related Web links: online-today.de—Online Today, for online rankings of various services and businesses (G); **landsend.de**—Lands' End Germany (G)

Die Post: Not Your Father's Post Office

Step into almost any German post office these days and you'll discover an entirely different place from what it was just a few years ago. Even before you enter *die Post*, the location itself speaks volumes about how radically this German institution has changed. The new modern black-and-yellow lighted Deutsche Post signs are seen increasingly in German shopping arcades. The traditional large central post office is giving way to many more conveniently located branches in places where Germans never saw a post office before.

Once you're inside, more indications of change become apparent. Instead of the former multitude of windows that were each designated for different postal services, Germany's recently privatized Deutsche Post AG now offers a multitude of services from any window. Customers can also order cellular telephone (*das Handy*) service, buy wrapping materials, and even pick up a greeting card to accompany the package. Rows of once hard-to-find post office boxes (*Postfach*) line the entryway. It's definitely not your father's post office anymore!

Although German post offices have always offered postal banking and telephone services, these are now presented in a more businesslike and attractive manner that reflects the splitting up of the former government-run Bundespost's three divisions: the mail (*die gelbe Post*, "yellow post"), telecommunications (now run by the separate Deutsche Telekom AG), and postal banking. Although that split and privatization began in 1995, the dramatic changes are just now becoming apparent countrywide.

Related Web link: deutschepost.de—German post office (G)

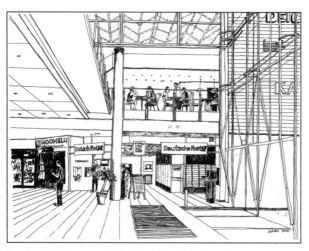

Here is a typical German post office in a modern shopping center.

E-Commerce.de

Do Germans shop on the Web? German entrepreneurs have traditionally been a rare breed. In fact, they were a largely non-existent species until the 1990s and then not a serious force until around mid-1999. Even as the Internet/Web business-and-entertainment phenomenon mushroomed in the United States and across the newly wired world, Germans were slow to jump onto the World Wide Web bandwagon. Although they were at the European fore-front on the Web, several factors kept Germany a distant third (behind the United States and Japan) in Internet usage. The first was a factor present in most of the world outside of the United States and Canada: per-minute online charges. Germans, like most of their European neighbors, had to pay telephone charges for every minute they were online, even if they reached their Internet service provider via a local phone call. The second limiting factor was the traditional German reluctance to use credit cards, whether in a bricks-and-mortar store or the online variety.

Granted, there were a few notable German E-entrepreneurial exceptions, including the business-software giant SAP, which had sprung up in Waldorf, Germany. Until the very late 1990s, however, such things were as rare as a non-beer-drinking Bavarian. True, a modest German version of Silicon Valley had formed in Munich, but Germany faced such a shortage of Net-savvy people and software programmers that a special (and controversial) "green card" was created to import foreign talent from as far away as India.

This is not to say that there haven't been German online success stories, but many have either disappeared or been swallowed up by bigger fish. An early German pioneering online bookseller, ABC-Bücherdienst, of Regensburg, was taken over by Amazon to become Amazon.de. However, Germany continues to be Europe's leading country on the Internet, and despite some problems.

Percent of People 16+ with Internet Access (Q1-2001)

COUNTRY	% AT HOME	% AT WORK
Austria	42	27
France	22	17
Germany	35	22
Sweden	61	41
Switzerland	43	31
United Kingdom	46	26

Percent of People 16+ Who Browse and Purchase Online

COUNTRY	% WHO BROWSE	% WHO PURCHASE
Austria	25	12
France	12	6
Germany	22	11
Sweden	46	26
Switzerland	32	17
United Kingdom	19	11

Source: AC Nielsen/Netratings

Related Web links: bundesregierung.de— German government on the Web, search for "E-commerce" for recent articles and statistics (E, G); t-online.de—Deutsche Telekom (G)

Questions You Should Ask—Part 1

Here are three questions you should ask yourself before leaving for Germany:

1. Will my credit or ATM cards work in Germany? Most major credit cards (Visa, MasterCard, or American Express) are accepted for purchases in shops and restaurants that accept credit cards at all (rarer than in much of the rest of the world). At ATMs, which are common in Germany, look for the Cirrus or Star logos, and your card will be accepted by most of those machines. Three caveats: (1) debit/ATM cards will work only with a checking account, not savings; (2) German ATMs accept only numerical PINs; (3) U.S. bank checks are virtually impossible to cash in Europe. Leave your checkbook at home. An ATM bonus: even with the extra international exchange fee that most credit card issuers charge (but don't itemize in your bill), you will usually get a more favorable rate of exchange by using a card rather than traveler's checks.

2. Will my cell/wireless telephone (*das Handy*) work in Germany? This depends on where you're coming from. If you live in North America, your normal wireless phone will not work in the land of *das Handy*. (Special international multiband phones are available through AT&T, Nextel, and other wireless providers.) If you live in the United Kingdom, in most of Western Europe, or in another country that uses the GSM digital wireless standard, your current mobile phone will probably work in German Europe. If you want a mobile phone during a visit, it is usually cheaper to buy a prepaid German *Handy* once you're there rather than renting a GSM phone or paying the charges for calls on an international wireless phone. (See the "Science and Technology" chapter for more details.)

3. How about electricity and appliances? German electricity comes in the 220-volt, 50-hertz (cycle) variety, which will destroy most North American 110-volt appliances without a voltage converter. Coming from most other non-Continental countries, you will also need a plug adapter for the German *Schukostecker* (safety plug) with their round prongs. Clocks, turntables, and other 60-hertz devices will not work properly in Germany because of the 10-cycles-per-second difference. For other large and small appliances, you can get transformers (*Transformatoren*) that will convert the voltage. North American television sets are not compatible with the German PAL TV system.

Related Web links: visa.de—Visa Deutschland (G); visa.com—(E); german-way.com/german/ handy.html—information about using cell phones in Germany (E); mastercard.com (E); eurocard.de (G)

Questions You Should Ask—Part 2

Here are four questions you should ask yourself in Germany:

1. Why are Germans so pushy? They don't seem to know what a line/queue is. This "pushy" behavior is not limited to Germans. It's a European thing. The European tendency for public aggression is also seen on the road. It means the meek will wait forever. When there's an opening, go for it. If you don't, a German will. This applies to getting on the bus or getting out of a traffic circle. You need to adjust to a different mentality that regards politeness as a sign of weakness, and regards smiling for no reason as a sign of a weak mind. One of the few locations where Germans will actually stand in line is at an ATM (*der Geldautomat*).

2. Why are Germans such fanatics when it comes to banning loud noise? This is a country with laws that prohibit mowing your lawn on Sunday or playing your piano after 8:00 P.M. . . . all in the cause of noise prevention. The reason is simple: excessive noise violates the sacred German right to privacy. A German's home is not only his or her castle—it's a private preserve. In a country with high population density and close living conditions, such laws are regarded as essential to civil order. Other signs of Germans' sacred privacy: closed doors, front-yard fences, and less use of first names.

3. Why should I take along my own shopping bag when I go out to buy groceries and many other items? Most Ger-man grocery stores and many other shops offer plastic or cloth bags, but for a price. They're usually not free. The majority of German shoppers automatically take their own *Einkaufstasche* to avoid paying extra for a store bag. To add insult to injury, you usually have to bag your own groceries! German checkers have it pretty soft; they also get to sit at the register while you're bagging the groceries they just rang up.

4. What does "GEZ" mean, and why do I have to pay it? German public radio and television are financed through a fee charged for the use of a radio or television set. The initials stands for Gebühreneinzugszentrale der Rundfunkanstalten, which is roughly the "central broadcasting fee agency" that collects what is essentially a tax on your television set and radio to help pay for the commercial-free programs broadcast by ARD and ZDF, the two public broadcasting networks. You can get the GEZ forms at banks, at post offices, or online (see link below) Yes, there is a fine if you get caught not paying your GEZ fees, and you can't get out of it by claiming you watch only commercial television.

Related Web link: gez.de (G)—Pay your GEZ fees online

Rules for Dealing with Germans

Everyone is *not* alike!

1. Remember that Germans really hate rule breakers!

2. Germans and Americans do *not* think and act alike in social and business situations—especially in first encounters. Get over the myth that "we're all basically alike." It sounds good, but this mind-set is counterproductive.

3. Germans tend to be blunt, frank, and—to Anglo-American eyes—tactless in certain situations. They tend to correct you when you don't want to be corrected. That's because they are primarily concerned with exchanging facts and information, not "warm fuzziness." Since they also do this with other Germans, try to understand that you have not been singled out for special treatment.

4. Germans aren't into "idle chatter." They don't really care if you "have a nice day" (an expression they view as a symbol of American "superficiality"), and they don't want to talk about (a) their jobs, (b) their kids or family, or (c) the weather with a stranger (i.e., anyone they haven't known for at least a year or more). Such conversation is reserved for close friends.

5. Both the German language and the Germans draw a clear line between *Freunde* (*du/ihr*) and *Bekannte* (*Sie*), between private (home) and public (work). You are a *Bekannte(r)* ("acquaintance") and on *Sie* terms until your German counterpart says

otherwise. This is one of the most difficult rules for easygoing, just-call-me-Bob Americans to truly grasp and internalize.

6. Germans have been known to smile, but unnecessary smiling is frowned on. A German needs a good reason to smile. In fact, excessive smiling for most Europeans is an indication of weak-mindedness. Don't overdo smiling around Germans. At heart, Germans are pessimists, and they enjoy their pessimism. Don't deprive them of that pleasure. Corollary to Rule 6: Never try to tell a joke in German. Leave this to professionals like Harald Schmidt (a well-known German night-show host) or Germans who have had too much to drink. Germans have a sense of humor, but it has no resemblance to either the American or British variety. It takes many years to delve into the German sense of humor.

7. Learn and accept Rules 1 through 6. Don't think you can (or should) change people. Learn to adjust to *them*, rather than expecting them to adjust to you. If you react with indignation or anger, even privately, then you are displaying a profound lack of understanding of the culture in which you're trying to function.

There are a few Germans who don't fit the preceding rules, but all six of them are now living in the United States or Canada.

Related Web link: german-way.com/german—
see *Contents* for The Expat Page and Interviews
with Expats (E)

Sie and *Du*: You and Thou Shouldn't Get Too Familiar

The rule for *you* in German is simple: When in doubt, use the formal *Sie*. Addressing a person as *du* when *Sie* would be correct is demeaning and expresses—whether you mean to or not—either an air of superiority or unwarranted familiarity on your part. Neither will help you win any German friends.

This little language detail is not as minor as English speakers may tend to think. Although the English form of *du*—*thou*—died out of English, it is alive and well in German and the other European languages. For some reason, the familiar *thou* of English faded away, while *du*, *tœ*, *tu*, and other familiar-*you* forms continue to be used in German, Spanish, French, and Italian. This distinction between the familiar *you* and the formal *you* serves a function that English speakers should not ignore. While *thou* is now seen only in poetry, the Bible, Shakespeare, and other sources of "olde English," its German equivalent serves an important role in modern German. The German equivalent of "ya'll" or "you guys" is *ihr*, the plural form of *du*.

To better understand this concept, relate it to similar situations in English. We may no longer have *thou*, but when talking to, for instance, Robert Johnson, we do address him as "Mr. Johnson" when "Bob" isn't appropriate—and this is more often the case in German than in English! Even though Americans may use first names before they know someone's last name, the fact is that under certain conditions, addressing someone as "Mr." or "Mrs." is the right thing to do. Germans use *Sie*—the formal *you*—to accomplish this social acknowledgment. White-collar workers generally use *Sie*. In fact, Germans who have worked together in the same office for many years will often continue to address each other as *Sie*.

Blue-collar workers, on the other hand, use *du*. This familiar form of *you* is also used by members of certain other social groups, such as students and soldiers. Likewise, the familiar *du* is common among family members; between good friends; and for children, God, and pets. Although there has been a tendency among the younger generation to use *du* sooner and more often than their elders, this is not always the case. To avoid those unfortunate miscues, it is wise to wait for your German friends (*Freunde*) and acquaintances (*Bekannte*) to initiate the use of *du*—remembering that Germans make a clear distinction between *Freunde* and *Bekannte*.

Related Web link: german.about.com—German language (E, G)

"Fräulein" or "Frau"? "*Du*" or "*Sie*"?

Only in Germany would you find a 2,000-word newspaper essay on the dilemma of how to address a waitress in a restaurant. A recent article in the *Frankfurter Rundschau* reflects an aspect of German culture that is sometimes difficult for Germans, much less *Ausländer*, to understand: the various levels of formality or informality (mixed in with political correctness) reflected in the German language.

At some point in the early 1970s as the *Frauenbewegung* (women's movement) was taking hold, it became a faux pas to try to get your waitress's attention by shouting out, "*Fräulein!*" (FROY-line, "Miss!"). Any woman above the age of about 18, married or not, could no longer be addressed as "Miss." Rather than adopt a new word like the English term *Ms.*, German logically proclaimed that henceforth, just as *Herr* (Mr.) applied to any adult male, the existing title *Frau* (Mrs.) would apply to any adult woman, including waitresses. This elegantly avoided the "Ms." problem that still plagues English. Soon, however, Germans realized that they had created a new problem. While it had been socially acceptable to shout "*Fräulein*" across a room filled with diners, no respectable German woman was going to put up with being addressed as simply "*Frau*" without her last name. It just sounds so wrong in German!

So, now Germans are still faced with the addressing-the-waitress dilemma. Neither the German Hotel and Restaurant Association (DEHOGA) nor the Association of Hotel and Service Personnel has been able to suggest a good alternative.

Some restaurants have adopted the once radical idea of putting American-style name tags on their waitresses. (This in a culture that sees no problem in two people who have worked together in an office for 15 years still calling each other "Mr. So-and-so" or "Mrs. So-and-so" rather than using their first names.) The name tags allow patrons to call a waitress by her last name: "*Frau Schmidt!*" Some restaurants have even been using first-name tags, a most un-German thing to do!

Related Web link: dehoga.de—German hospitality industry home page (E, G)

Clothes and Fashion: Casual, Formal, or Traditional?

Despite famous German fashion designers such as Karl Lagerfeld, Jil Sander, Hugo Boss, and Wolfgang Joop, and fashion models such as Claudia Schiffer, Heidi Klum, and Nadja Auermann, everyday Germans don't exactly have a reputation as fashion plates. This fact has prompted some of the fashion icons mentioned to criticize their countrymen for their lack of fashion sense, and most of these German designers work primarily in non-German places such as Milan, Paris, or New York.

Back in their homeland, most Germans—male and female—go to school and work in blue jeans and other very casual attire. Even the teachers and professors often look as casual as their pupils or more so. Most German males consider "dressed up" to be wearing a sports coat or blazer without a tie, although those employed by banks and some other companies generally do wear suits and ties to work. Management tends to dress more formally than labor, but in many cases fashion also reflects German society's nonelitist frame of mind, and it is virtually impossible to see any authority-level differences in what someone is wearing.

When Germans buy clothing, they generally pay higher prices than those seen in Anglo-American stores. However, clothes and shoes are expected to last a long time. The German thinks it's better to buy fewer, good-quality clothes than a lot of cheaper items that will quickly wear out.

You may be in Germany for a long time before you see the stereotypical German wearing lederhosen (which means "leather pants") or a dirndl, a traditional southern German/Austrian dress. Nevertheless, there are times when such *Trachten*, or folk costumes, are worn, and specialty shops sell such items. These traditional fashions are not inexpensive, but they are expected to last a lifetime.

Related Web Links: vogue.de—see *Society, Who Is Who*, for information on Wolfgang Joop, Karl Lagerfeld, Jil Sander, and Claudia Schiffer (G); hugo-boss.de—Hugo Boss corporate website (E, G); lederhosenmuseum.de—Virtual Lederhosen Museum (E, G); tyrol-international.com for lederhosen and dirndl purchases (E, G); deutscheshaus.cc for German products (E)

Das Bad or *das WC*? Germans Don't "Go to the Bathroom"!

There are three essential facts to know about this delicate subject: (1) the German terms for *men/gentlemen* and *ladies*, (2) the difference between a bathroom and a toilet, and (3) how to ask where the "rest room" is.

First of all, the German language is more direct and uses far fewer euphemisms than English when it comes to basic bodily functions in general and to the place for "relieving oneself" in particular. In German, you call a toilet a toilet (*eine Toilette, das* WC). It's not a "rest" room, a "powder" room, the "loo," or the "john"—it's the room with a toilet, *die Toilette*. The closest German comes to toilet euphemisms are words borrowed from English: *das* WC, short for "water closet" and pronounced VAY-SAY, or the somewhat less refined *das Klo*. On the autobahn and in some public places, you'll also see the symbol "00" (*null, null*). Generally, but not always, "00" means an outhouse-style, hole-in-the-ground, waterless type of toilet, whereas "WC" always denotes a flush toilet.

The toilet is certainly never the bathroom! If you go to the "bathroom" in Germany, it is to take a bath. Although *das amerikanische Badezimmer* has gained favor over the years in German homes, hotels, and other places, the traditional German approach has long been to separate the two activities by locating them in different rooms. The "bath" or "bathing" room is called, logically, *das Badezimmer* or *das Bad*. It contains a bathtub (*die Badewanne*) and/or a shower (*die Dusche*) but usually no toilet. The toilet or water closet may be located in its own room next door or even farther down the hall. So, if you inquire of your German host, "*Wo ist das Badezimmer?*" you are likely to get a somewhat startled look that asks, "You want to take a bath now?" If you want to use the facilities, just ask: "*Wo ist die Toilette, bitte?*" In public places, the ladies' room is marked "*Damen*" or "D," the men's room "*Herren*" or "H." Most German public toilets have an attendant, who expects a tip to be left in the dish strategically placed near the exit. Also, it is wise, particularly for women, to carry some change for pay toilet stalls, which are common in Germany.

"*Wo der Kaiser auch zu Fuss geht*" is one of the few euphemistic toilet expressions in German. It refers to "where even the emperor has to walk" and is used in a humorous way rather than to avoid the actual word *toilet*. A shorter version is simply "*Ich muss wohin*" ("I must go there [where the emperor . . .]"). Other ways to say you've gotta go: *Ich muss . . . aufs Klo/auf die Toilette/aufs WC*.

This is a typical German hotel bathroom, complete with toilet and bidet.

Weights and Measures: Give 'em an Inch and They'll Take a Meter

When the $125 million Mars Climate Orbiter apparently burned up in the Martian atmosphere in September 1999, it was a spectacular example of how confusion over different systems of weights and measures can lead to problems. The orbiter met its fiery fate only because the scientists had mistakenly fed it data calculated in British pounds instead of the metric newtons (units of force) that the spacecraft's computer was expecting.

The Anglo-American system of weights and measures makes its last stand in the United States and, to a lesser degree, in Great Britain. The English system itself varies from country to country in the former British Empire, often in mysterious ways. For purposes of conversion, the following table compares the U.S. version of the Anglo-American system, since the United States is about the only place the older system is still being used in everyday life.

Germany and the rest of Europe use the metric system that was first proposed in France in 1791 before gradually being accepted throughout the civilized world—that is, everywhere but in the former American colonies. Even there, both the U.S. yard and pound were legally defined in metric terms after 1893. In Europe, too, there are a few measurement oddities. For instance, TV screen measurements and tire sizes for cars and bikes are expressed in inches (*Zoll*), not centimeters. Also, horsepower (*Pferdestärke*), rather than the official watts or joules, continues to be used commonly in Germany and elsewhere.

These international measurement differences become more than abstract math problems when an American starts looking for a 150-square-meter apartment in Germany (150 *Quadratmeter* × 10.7641 square feet = 1,614.615 square feet) On the road, it is relatively simple to convert kilometers to miles or vice versa, but it can be a nightmare trying to convert miles per gallon to *Liter auf 100 Kilometer*. That's why we offer the following conversion charts.

Temperature

FAHRENHEIT	CENTIGRADE
230	110
212	100
(boiling point of water)	
194	90
176	80
158	70
140	60
122	50
104	40
98.4	37
(normal body temperature)	
86	30
70	21
(room temperature)	

FAHRENHEIT	CENTIGRADE
68	20
50	10
32	0
(freezing point of water)	
14	−10
−4	−20
−22	−30
−40	−40

Miles per Gallon (MPG)/*Liter auf 100 Kilometer* (L/100 KM)

MPG	L/100 KM	L/100 KM	MPG
20	11.761	10	23.5
25	9.409	9	26.13
30	6.72	8	29.40
35	6.72	7	33.60
40	5.88	6	39.20

Related Web links: webmath.com/convert .html—Webmath metric converters (E); worldwidemetric.com—see *Metric Conversion Calculators* (E); souprecipe.com/conversions .asp; recipe.com (E)

This depicts Wednesday, August 2 at 2:38 P.M. on a German clock and calendar.

16 *Länder*, 16 School Systems

The German educational system follows the European model of free public education and a variety of secondary schools for academic and vocational education, rather than the American model of a single comprehensive high school for all students. However, as in the United States, educational matters in Germany are primarily the responsibility of each of the 16 states, or *Länder*. The 16 state systems are coordinated to some extent by the federal German Ständige Konferenz der Kultusminister (Standing Conference of Education Ministers) and a 1971 agreement (Hamburger Abkommen) among the *Länder* that created a higher degree of uniformity in a system that at one time had students starting the school year in the spring in some states, and in the fall in others.

With reunification in 1990, Germany had to solve the problem of integrating the former Communist East German school system of the five "New States" into the existing system of the Federal Republic. Students in the eastern German states, for instance, still graduate after 12 years of schooling, versus 13 years in most of the western states. Also, most schools in the East still have a lunch cafeteria, while most in the West do not.

Germany requires 12 years of schooling, from age 6 to 18. Just how and in which kind of school those years are spent depends on whether a student chooses an academic or a vocational (*Berufschule*) track. In any case, the German constitution (*Grundgesetz*) makes religious instruction a compulsory subject in German schools, though parents and students may opt out when the student reaches a certain age.

Since kindergarten (children's garden) is a German invention, it may be surprising to learn that kindergarten is usually not a part of the German public school system, and attendance is voluntary. Most German kindergartens are run by churches or other nonprofit organizations. Some are even company sponsored. In the East, however, the so-called *Kinderkrippen* preschools are still part of the school system. Although kindergarten has traditionally been popular, and more than 65 percent of kindergarten-age children enroll, it wasn't until 1996 that all German parents attained the legal right to have their children attend kindergarten.

At age six, all German children go to *Grundschule*, usually grades one through four. After that, there are many secondary school choices: *Hauptschule* (five to six years of general education), *Realschule* (six-year academic curriculum), *Gesamtschule* (comprehensive curriculum), or *Gymnasium* (nine-year academic curriculum). Students who wish to attend a university must graduate with an *Abitur* school-leaving certificate, usually from a *Gymnasium*.

Related Web link: schulweb.de—German schools online (G)

School Choice: *Wer die Wahl Hat, Hat die Qual.*
(He Who Has a Choice Has Torture.)

When Americans debate the issue of school choice, they may want to take a look at the German education system. It is a system of many choices, including not only *which* school to attend but also which *kind* of school to attend. While the German school system has some problems of its own, one of them is not lack of choice.

German students and their parents have an almost bewildering array of options when it comes to education. In fact, one criticism of the German "multi-school" system is that it forces students and parents to make such important choices too early. In most *Länder* (education is a state matter, not a federal matter, in Germany), students must pass exams and decide after their fourth school year, at the tender age of 10, whether they will attend a *Hauptschule*, a *Realschule*, a *Gesamtschule*, or a *Gymnasium*. (There are *Sonderschulen* for special education.) Each of the secondary-school categories has a different course of study and a different educational goal. (See the table.) Although alternatives are possible — including the so-called orientation phase in grades five and six, which allows students to switch schools in the seventh grade, and the *zweiter Bildungsweg* (sec-

ond educational path) of evening remedial schools — the German system is fairly rigid once a path has been chosen.

Partly in response to this inflexibility, some states introduced the *Gesamtschule*, or comprehensive high school, in the 1960s. But the *Gesamtschule*, which combines the three traditional school types under one roof, has met with limited success in only a few *Länder*. It has been associated with a lowering of standards, particularly for earning an *Abitur*, the vital German secondary school diploma required for university study. While in the 1970s, only about 11 percent of students graduated with an *Abitur* and went on to a university, in the 1990s, that figure had climbed to 34 percent.

Whichever kind of school the student chooses to attend, he or she can opt for almost any school in the community. German schools compete with each other for students, and Germany's outstanding public transportation system makes it possible for students to attend a school on the other side of town from where they live. Of course, a student may or may not be accepted by a school and may have to choose an alternative.

Type of School	Age Range	Certification Awarded
Hauptschule	10–15	*Hauptschulabschluss*
Realschule	10–16	*Realschulabschluss*
Gymnasium	10–19	*Abitur*
Berufsaufbauschule (integrated)	16–17	*Fachhochschulreife*
Fachoberschule (specialized)	16–18	*Fachhochschulreife*
Fachschule (technical)	16–18	*Fachhochschulreife*
Berufsfachschule (vocational)	16–18	*Fachhochschulreife*

The German University Crisis

The German university system is very different from the Anglo-American system. One of the biggest contrasts is that German (and Austrian) university students pay absolutely no tuition fees. Their only costs are for books and room and board. As critics have pointed out, sometimes you get what you pay for.

While the entire German educational system, from preschool to college, is facing an identity crisis, it is the colleges and universities (*Hochschulen*) that face the biggest challenges and the most criticism. The ongoing crisis of German higher education has been making headlines for many years, but meaningful change has been slow in coming. Despite the massive student riots of 1968 and more recent protests in 1997, German *Studenten* still confront the overcrowded lecture halls, uninspired teaching, and numerous other ills that inspired this 1996 headline in the German news magazine *Focus*: "Disappointed students, helpless politicians: the university needs more competition."

Since Germany has virtually no private universities, from where is the competition supposed to come? This almost total lack of private universities with their alumni and foundation funding, so common in the Anglo-American college system, is the result of a long-standing German aversion to dreaded "elitism." Because all German *Unis* are supposed to be equal, they all tend to be mediocre, as well as much more provincial and far less international than in many other countries.

In the last few years, a couple of noble experiments have arisen to try to shake up the German higher education establishment, but, again, with only limited success.

More recently, the International University Bremen (IUB) opened in 2001 with 130 students in former military barracks to establish the private and international Alfred Krupp College. The IUB intended to enroll a student body comprising no more than 50 percent Germans, but it had trouble attracting even that number. The city-state of Bremen invested 230 million marks in this experimental college that is supposed to encourage competition and attract some 1,200 students within four years.

Will such efforts by two of Germany's 300 universities and technical institutes bring results? Considering the titles of two recent German books on the topic, progress can't come too soon. Nevertheless, since their publication in the late 1990s, neither *Rotten to the Core? (Im Kern verrotet?)* nor *Can the University Be Saved? (Ist die Uni noch zu retten?)* has forced the *Universitäten* or German legislators to make any serious reforms.

Related Web links: daad.de—Deutscher Akademischer Austauschdienst (DAAD) (G); **daad.org**—German Academic Exchange Service, same as the DAAD but in English (E); **uni-karlsruhe.de**—*Uni Karlsruhe*, almost any German university website can be found by using a link similar to this one if you have the city or university name (G); **campus-germany.de**—All about study in Germany (E, G)

From Novel to Screenplay: Austria and Germany as a Source for Hollywood

Few filmgoers are aware of it, but Hollywood has quite a record of drawing on German, Austrian, or Swiss sources for its movies, both past and present. One of the latest, Stanley Kubrick's controversial *Eyes Wide Shut* (1999), was based on Arthur Schnitzler's book *Traumnovelle*, an Austrian work from the 1920s. While Schnitzler's erotic novella was set in fin de siècle Vienna, Kubrick's screenplay moved the characters to turn-of-the-century New York in the 1990s.

Kubrick is just one of many filmmakers who throughout the years have borrowed, adapted, and stolen material originally written in German. From Walt Disney to Miramax, from *Bambi* to *The Parent Trap*, Hollywood has often gone to the Germanic well for movie material. While the films may be famous, the original Austrian and German authors generally are not. Besides obvious borrowings, such as *The Sound of Music* (1965), based on the true-life story of the Austrian von Trapp family, many familiar Hollywood productions are derived from unfamiliar sources.

Vicki Baum (1888–1960), born Hedwig Baum in Vienna, wrote the novel *Menschen im Hotel* in 1929, which later became a play and film. MGM's *Grand Hotel* (1932) starred Greta Garbo, John Barrymore, and Joan Crawford. After 1933, Baum settled in Los Angeles, where she continued to write (after 1941 in English).

Another Austrian, Felix Salzmann (1869–1945), who wrote under the name Felix Salten, is the author of *Bambi: A Life in the Woods* (1923), *Bambi's Children*, and other animal tales. Few fans of Disney's 1942 animated classic *Bambi* have ever heard of Salten. The studio never really publicized his contribution to Disney's hit. Salten was living in Switzerland at the time of his death, only three years after *Bambi*'s release.

Disney was not much more forthcoming when the studio released another hit film in 1961. *The Parent Trap* featured Hayley Mills in the dual role of twin sisters separated by the divorce of their parents. The film was based on a book by the German author Erich Kästner, *Das doppelte Lottchen*. In Kästner's book, Luise and Lotte (played by real twin sisters in a 1950 German film version) pull their identity switch in Munich and Vienna. The latest Hollywood version, released in 1998, remains true to the tale-of-two-countries idea, transforming Germany and Austria into the United States and the United Kingdom.

Disney also used another Kästner story (and an earlier 1931 German film) for its 1964 *Emil and the Detectives*, which was actually filmed in Germany.

Related Web link: german-way.com/cinema— more on the German-Hollywood connection (E)

Going to the Movies: *Wir Gehen ins Kino*

With the global spread of the multiscreen "cineplex" and Hollywood's world domination of cinematic entertainment, going to the movies (*ins Kino gehen*) in the Western world is pretty much the same experience anywhere—except for the language.

In Germany and Austria, non-German movies are almost always dubbed (*synchronisiert*) into German. (The Swiss, dealing with three major languages, tend to use subtitles, *Untertiteln*.) Because about 70 to 85 percent of the motion pictures that Germans watch in a given year still come from Hollywood and other non-German studios, dubbing is big business, with the voices of certain German actors regularly standing in for famous Hollywood stars. With a resurgence of German film production in recent years, movies made in Germany have been capturing a larger percentage of the box office. German cinematic hits such as *Lola rennt* (in English, *Run Lola Run*) and the comedy *Der Schuh des Manitu* (*Manitu's Shoe*) have been able to appeal to German filmgoers who had shunned homeland productions in the past. (*Run Lola Run* star Franka Potente has even enjoyed some success in Hollywood with *Blow* and *The Bourne Identity*.) *Manitu* managed to do something no German film had done in a long time: reach number one and stay in the top three for many weeks.

However, larger German cities such as Berlin, Frankfurt, Hamburg, and Munich have cinemas that regularly show English-language films with the original soundtrack. German newspaper and Web movie listings indicate these with either the designation "OV" (*Originalfassung*, "original version"), "O-Ton" (for "original soundtrack"), or "OmU" (*Originalfassung mit Untertiteln*, "original with subtitles"). Films on video and DVD are also frequently available with an English soundtrack. European DVD titles, in particular, are usually released with soundtracks in several languages, including English, with a wide choice of subtitle languages. (Caution: European videos, DVDs, and television broadcasts are not compatible with North American players or receivers.)

One more note about movies in Germany: motion pictures are released worldwide at different times in various countries. In part, this is because of the time lag caused by dubbing, but it is also the result of a Hollywood marketing ploy designed to spread out a movie's box-office staying power.

Related Web links: cinemaxx.de—*Cinemaxx,* a large German movie theater chain, at whose site you can find films now showing in cinemas all over Germany (G); **film.de**—film listings, ratings, news, DVDs, and more (G); **kino.de**—movie news, background stories, and film listings (G); **kino-berlin.de**—find any movie now playing in Berlin, including OmU and OV movies in English (G); **kinonews.de**—a film and entertainment news site with an online movie-ticket service (G); **cinema.de**—Cinema Online, the Web version of Germany's largest movie magazine (G); **imdb.com**—Internet Movie Database lists German and English film titles and includes tons of information on actors, directors, films, and more (not all of which is always accurate) (E, G)

Mel Gibson appears to be wearing a crown above this German ad kiosk.

Popular Music *auf Deutsch*: From the Ärzte to Rammstein

The modern German sound of music is rarely heard outside of German Europe. Although there have been a few notable exceptions over the years, including some hit songs ("99 Luftballons" by Nena, "Rock Me Amadeus" by Falco) and some groups (Kraftwerk in the 1970s and Rammstein today), German rock and rap groups are largely unknown outside the German-speaking world.

Thanks to Germany's home market of 82 million people (plus another 10 million or so in Austria and German Switzerland), German-language musical artists can survive and even prosper by performing exclusively in their own language. But when you listen to the popular music coming out of the radio in Germany, you may feel as if you were in Britain or the United States, since the majority of songs have English lyrics. Even German and other European groups usually record their songs in English because the market is so huge.

Notwithstanding, a number of well-known German and Austrian artists refuse to "sell out" by writing songs *mit englischen Texten*. You may never have heard of the Ärzte, Die Prinzen, Herbert Grönemeyer, Die Fantastischen Vier, Udo Lindenberg, or Marius Müller Westernhagen, but their popular songs in German are well known to almost any German under the age of 40. Although some of these artists have dipped their toes into English waters at least once, most never did or quickly came back to the German shore.

One example of a German musician who has tried English but stuck with German is the cultural icon Udo Lindenberg.

Born in 1946, Lindenberg has crossed several generations with his satirical soft-rock social commentary and is still going strong. It was Udo who provoked the East German Communist chief Erich Honecker with songs entitled *"Sonderzug nach Pankow"* (which translates to "special train to Pankow," a city in what was then East Berlin, sung to the tune of "Chattanooga Choo-Choo") and also *"Generalsekretär,"* which featured a music video showing a cartoon Honecker high-jumping over the Berlin Wall.

Herbert Grönemeyer, another perennial favorite, is virtually unknown in the English-speaking world, despite his prominent role as the war correspondent aboard the U-boat in *Das Boot*—the most successful German movie prior to *Run Lola Run*. He has recorded more than a dozen albums in German and does sold-out concert tours all over German Europe.

Give German music a try! You may like the sound.

Related Web links: falco.at—although Falco is no longer with us, his website is (E); **smudo .com**—Fanta4, some streaming audio sound clips available (G); **groenemeyer.de**—Herbert Grönemeyer, more than a dozen CD albums (G); **kraftwerk.com**—their techno sounds started in the 1970s (G); **nena.de**—99 red balloons and all that (G); **dieprinzen.de**—Die Prinzen, a group from eastern Germany (G); **rammstein.de**—not for everyone, but their heavy-metal sounds (in German) are also popular outside of Germany (G); **udo-lindenberg.de**—Udo Lindenberg (G); **laut.de**—a German music site (G)

Der Wein: A Brief German Wine Guide

German wines in general are the Rodney Dangerfield of the wine world. They tend not to get the respect reserved for French or even better California wines. The reasons are complex but in part have been self-inflicted. In the 1960s and 1970s, German vintners created a bad image for themselves when they exported crate upon crate of sugary sweet wines known as Blue Nun, Schwarze Katz, and Liebfraumilch, which long overshadowed the finer wines that Germany produces. Germany further shot itself in the foot by refusing to allow its wine makers to indicate on their labels the growing location (*Lage*) of the grapes used for a particular vintage's production. Labels may indicate the district, or *Anbaugebiet*, but that is a more general distinction than the *Lage*. Under German wine law, the label also provides a great deal of information about the grape harvest (six categories from early to late) and the sugar content (the Öchsle scale of sweetness or dryness). Unfortunately, none of these label criteria has anything to do with the quality of the wine—but they will tell you in detail just how sweet (*süß*) or dry (*trocken*) a given wine is.

Today, however, serious wine connoisseurs know that Germany (like Austria) produces some of the world's finest wines, white wines in particular. (Only approximately 10 percent of German production is red wine.) Germany's 13 wine regions from Ahr to Württemberg (and Austrian areas such as the Wachau, Neusiedlersee, and South Styria) produce many different wines of top quality. German wine by law is either *Tafelwein* (common table wine) or *Qualitätswein* (quality wine). This latter category is further divided into two sub-categories: *Qualitätswein bestimmter Anbaugebiete* (QbA), which is quality wine from a designated region, and *Qualitätswein mit Prädikat* (QmP), quality wine with special attributes, the highest category. A QmP wine may contain no added sugar, while a QbA wine is permitted to compensate for Germany's short, cool growing season with additional sugar. The label of a *Qualitätswein mit Prädikat* carries one of six *Prädikate* (attributes) that indicates the grape's degree of ripeness (and thus, sweetness) at harvest: *Kabinett* (first harvest, the driest), *Spätlese, Auslese, Beerenauslese, Eiswein*, and *Trockenbeerauslese* (the sweetest, from grapes dried on the vine). Most German wine is produced from the Riesling, Sylvaner, Müller-Thurgau, and Gewürztraminer grape varieties.

> **Prost!**
> The German equivalent of "Cheers" is *"Prost!"*

Related Web links: germanwine.de—German Wine (E, G); winepage.de—The German Wine Page by Peter Ruhrberg (E); austrian.wine .co.at—Austrian Wine (E, G)

FOOD AND DRINK
Brot und Wurst

*In der Not ißt man die Wurst auch ohne
Brot!*

(SPRICHWORT)

*In an emergency one even eats sausage
without bread!*

(PROVERB)

The two vital staples of the German diet
are bread (*Brot*) and sausage (*Wurst*).
Often served up together to create *ein
heißes Würstchen*, the Germanic equivalent of a hot dog, these are the two dietary
ingredients most associated with German
cooking, *deutsche Küche*. Only the beverage known as "liquid bread"—beer
(*Bier*)—can even come close in importance; sauerkraut is a distant fourth.
Despite the more recent invasion of
American fast food, Italian pizza, Turkish
Dörner Kebap, and other "foreign"
comestibles, the Germanic version of
McDonald's has long been the *Würstelbude*, *Würstchenstand*, or *Wurstmaxe*
(sausage stand). A *Currywurst* (diced
bratwurst with ketchup and curry powder)
could be called the German national
favorite.

The fact that there are more than 200
kinds of bread and 1,500 sausage varieties
illustrates the importance of these elements in the diet of people in the German-speaking world. Bread, in many shapes and
colors, is ever present in shops and restaurants and on dining tables. The *Bäckerei*
("bakery") has always been the one big
exception to Germany's strict laws concerning opening hours (*Ladenschluss*),
with bakeries allowed to open much earlier
than regular shops and stores in order to
provide the Germans, Austrians, and Swiss
with their fresh daily bread. They buy their
Brot in the form of rolls (*Brötchen, Semmeln*) or in a wide variety of loaves known
by so many names that it would be impossible to list most of them here. A few of the
more common terms are *Weissbrot* (white
bread), *Schwarzbrot* (dark bread), *Bauernbrot* (coarse rye bread), *Roggenbrot* (rye
bread), and *Salzstangel* (salted rolls).

Wurst Expressions and Sayings

Alles hat ein Ende, nur die Worst hat zwei.	Everything has an end; only the sausage has two.
Das ist mir Wurst.	It's all the same to me.
Es geht um die Wurst.	It's time to fish or cut bait.
kleines Würstchen	small-time operator, small-fry
Wurstblatt	a rag (in reference to a newspaper)
Wurstmaxe	sausage stand, vendor (derives from a Berlin vendor who called himself "*Akademischer Wurstmaxe*")
wurstig	indifferent, trifling, unimportant
Wurst wider Wurst	tit for tat

Related Web links: brot.de—Deutsches Brot provides photos of 25 kinds of German bread (G); **hueber.de/lerner/daf-beitraegel/currywurst.asp** —shows a survey of the popular dish known as Currywurst (G)

This German *Metzgerei* offers a multitude of sausage types.

Das Bier: From Bock to Lager

Both the German and the English words for the ancient beverage known as beer—the alcoholic refreshment made from barley and sometimes wheat and other grains—may be derived from the Anglo-Saxon word for barley, *baere*. That evolved into Old English *bere* and Old High German *bior*—and eventually into *beer* and *Bier*.

No one knows when or where the first beer or beerlike beverage was brewed, but it is likely that prehistoric cultures drank an alcoholic beverage made from fermented grains. Beer was an important drink in ancient cultures as diverse as the Egyptians, the Incas, the Sumerians, and the Chinese. In what is now Germany, the Germanic tribes were brewing a meadlike beer at least eight hundred years before the Romans arrived in northern Europe in the earliest days of the Christian era. It is known that the Germans were making a hops-flavored beer in the 11th century. By the 1200s, there was a thriving brewers' guild in Cologne (Köln).

In the earliest days of the beer trade, customers could not always be certain of the quality of the liquid they were drinking. In response, the German beer purity decree, the *Reinheitsgebot*, was promulgated in Bavaria in 1516. It simply listed certain price regulations and proclaimed the only ingredients allowed in the brewing process: barley, hops, yeast, and water. In 1906, the *Reinheitsgebot* became law, applying to all of Germany (but only for bottom-fermented, lager beers). The beer purity law is the world's oldest consumer-protection law still in effect.

German beers are brewed in many varieties. Lager beer's designation comes from the German word *lagern*, which means "to store." In the days before refrigeration, beer was usually brewed in the winter and stored for later consumption in the spring and summer—hence the term *lager*. In general, beer brewing is divided into two methods: top fermentation and bottom fermentation. The latter is used for lager beers and is an Austrian invention.

WORLD BEER CONSUMPTION—1999 (PER CAPITA)

1.	Czech Republic	160 liters
2.	Ireland	153 liters
3.	Germany	128 liters
4.	Austria	109 liters
5.	Luxembourg	107 liters
6.	Denmark	105 liters
7.	United Kingdom	99 liters
8.	Belgium	98 liters
9.	Australia	95 liters
10.	Slovakia	86 liters
11.	Netherlands	85 liters
12.	United States	84 liters

Source: Brewers Association of Japan

Related Web links: bier.de—German beer site (G); **german-way.com/german/beer.html**—more information on German beer (E)

Munich's Marienplatz (square) is in the heart of Bavaria, a noted beer-drinking region.

The Basics of Dining Out

Finding a Seat

Upon entering an Austrian, German, or Swiss dining establishment, do not wait to be seated. It could be a long wait. Diners are expected to find their own tables. Sometimes a food server may deign to suggest a table, but these employees are usually too busy ignoring the people who are already seated. If you see a sign (in German, of course) that says "Please wait to be seated," you have chosen an exclusive and probably expensive spot in which to dine. Most of the time, you just find your own seat.

The Kindness of Strangers

The German custom of sitting with perfect (or imperfect) strangers is actually very practical. The first time it happens can be a little unnerving for non-Europeans, but after a while, it makes a lot of sense. Europeans think it is a waste to let seats stay empty in a crowded restaurant just because you don't know the people sitting at a table. Once seated with strangers, you usually politely ignore each other. Sometimes the Germans may want to try out their English on you, but an American is no rarity in Germany.

No Free Lunch (Rolls)

Like most Americans, the Germans also believe there is no free lunch—or at least no free bread rolls. Feel free to partake, but the rolls aren't free. Nor is the butter; each pad is carefully counted. But before you show your American indignation, remember—there is no free lunch. Or dinner. In the States the rolls and butter are included

in the price of your meal. Because it's "free," you gobble up some rolls you may or may not really want. Europeans are more honest about it. You pay for what you consume. You really have to be hungry to eat rolls you know you're going to pay for.

Tipping

In German restaurants the tip (*Bedienung*, 15 percent) is already included in the bill, so don't overtip by adding another 10–15 percent. You don't leave the tip on the table as in the United States, but usually round up the bill to the nearest euro when you pay the waiter. If the service was very good or the bill is large, you should also add a small amount (5–7 percent) as an extra tip.

Related Web links: globalgourmet.com/destinations—delicious guides to German and Austrian dining (E); lib.uchicago.edu/keith/austria/restaurants.html—Keith Waclena's Austrian Restaurant Guide includes a good beer section (E); recipesource.com/ethnic/europe/german—extensive list of German recipes from the Searchable Online Archive of Recipes (E); ibmpcug.co.uk/~owls/edibilia.html—contains German recipes and useful links to German culinary sites (E); swr-online.de/grossmutter—see *Rezepte* for recipes from Vincent Klink, television cook (G)

You *Can* Drink the Water—Just Don't Do It in Public!

The tap water (*Leitungswasser, Trinkwasser*) in Germany ranks among the healthiest in the world. However, most Americans who somehow learned the German phrase for "Tap water, please." ("*Leitungswasser bitte.*") rarely use the phrase a second time. The puzzled look of disgust on the server's face is usually enough to discourage all but the most emboldened diner from making any second attempt. It is a look that says: "Ordinary water is fine for bathing, but only a barbarian would drink it!"

Why don't Germans drink perfectly safe water? Theories on this topic abound, but the reasons for their reluctance—more like a phobia—may go back to a time when public water sources were truly hazardous to your health. This tap-water angst is not just a German thing, either. Most other Europeans also avoid drinking tap water—except perhaps accidentally when they brush their teeth—despite its high quality. German drinking fountains are a rarity.

If you want to see stares of disbelief and horror, just pour yourself a glass of water from the kitchen sink in front of your German hosts. Their expressions alone will tell you that you have just violated some cardinal rule of German culture. Your shocked German friends may tell you that tap water is for washing the dishes and bathing, not for drinking. In a restaurant, if you ask for water (and you do have to ask!), it will come in a bottle and will usually be carbonated, *mit Gas* (if you don't want carbonated water, ask for *stilles Wasser*).

Another reason for *Trinkwasser-Angst* is the taste of some local water. While there are exceptions, much of the water coming out of German taps, despite its safety, just doesn't taste that good. Often *das Wasser* may be hard and heavily calcified (*verkalkt*—also a derogatory term applied to people), another reason for the popularity of filtered or bottled water.

Although beer, wine, coffee, tea, colas, and even fruit juice are certainly popular with Germans, the biggest-selling beverage remains good old *Mineralwasser* (sparkling mineral water)—a steadily rising trend over the last several decades. Germans drink more of the sparkling clear liquid per capita (in 2000) than any other beverage, including that German staple, beer—downing 101 liters of mineral water per person. (In 1970, the rate was only 12.5 liters per German.)

World Mineral Water Consumption—2000

1. Italy	155 liters
2. Mexico	136 liters
3. Belgium	123 liters
4. France	112 liters
5. Germany	101 liters
6. Spain	98 liters
7. Switzerland	95 liters

Source: Company reports, Verband Deutscher Mineralbrunnen

Related Web links: mineralwasser.com—Verband Deutscher Mineralbrunnen (G); **wasser.de**—Wasser.de (G); **fruchtsaft.de**—among other things, you'll learn that Germans drink more *Fruchtsaft*—fruit juice—than any of their European neighbors! (E, G)

A Baedeker on Baedeker and German Wanderlust

The *Wall Street Journal*'s article on what was in and out in the "new economy" was subtitled "An After-Bubble Baedeker: How to Be Really Cool as the Economy Chills." That 2001 headline dates back almost exactly 200 years to the birth of Karl Baedeker (1801–59), the German publisher whose name has become a synonym for any guidebook or travel guide.

Baedeker is the name of a German publishing house (*Verlag*) founded in Koblenz by Karl Baedeker in 1827. The famous "Baedeker system" was first established when Baedeker published the second edition of a guide to the Rhine between Mainz and Cologne. In that 1839 guidebook, he established the formula of practical and reliable information, keeping the Baedeker travel publications popular to the present day—and helped spawn many imitators. In his Rhine guide, Baedeker also introduced the use of star symbols to indicate attractions of special interest. The combination of German wanderlust and detailed travel information allowed the Baedeker guides to develop a large market of travel-hungry readers. It was a pioneering stage in the development of what we now call "tourism" and the "travel industry."

Baedeker's father was a printer and bookseller when Karl came into the world in the city of Essen on November 3, 1801. Karl continued that publishing tradition and earned a reputation for honesty and reliability by personally visiting and checking up on the locations and hotels mentioned in his books. After his death, his three sons expanded the operation by covering foreign destinations and publishing French and English editions. The first Baedeker guidebook in English appeared in 1861. The Karl Baedeker Verlag has since been located in Leipzig, Hamburg, and now Freiburg in Breisgau. The firm continues to publish its guides, including the automobile guides (Baedeker Autoverlag) added in 1952.

The following are selected English-language Baedeker titles in 1911:

- *Austria-Hungary*, including Dalmatia, Bosnia, Bucharest, Belgrade, and Montenegro—10 marks ($2.50 U.S.)
- *The Dominion of Canada*, with Newfoundland and an excursion to Alaska—6 marks ($1.50 U.S.)
- *Palestine and Syria*, including the principal routes through Mesopotamia and Babylonia—12 marks ($3.00 U.S.)
- *The United States*, with excursions to Mexico, Cuba, Puerto Rico, and Alaska—15 marks ($3.50 U.S.)

(Note: Exchange rates are approximate and are based on the "Money Table" that appeared in the Baedeker guides in 1911.)

Related Web link: baedeker.de—Baedeker official site (G)

Ötzi and Andreas Hofer: The Mummy and the Martyr

The summer of 1991 is fading into autumn. High in the Alps of Südtirol—South Tyrol, the German-speaking region of northern Italy—at an icy spot on the Hauslabjoch (ridge) just 100 yards from the Austrian border, a German hiking couple make a gruesome discovery. Partially visible in the melting glacial ice is what appears to be a human body. When Austrian authorities arrived on the scene, at first they believed they were dealing with one more unfortunate mountain climber. After all, the *Gendarmerie* routinely recover the corpses of ill-fated climbers every summer. But, the frozen remains were astounding: the naturally mummified body of a Stone Age man who died 5,300 years ago.

Archaeologists and researchers would later be horrified over the brutal, unscientific extrication of the oldest intact human remains ever found. Nevertheless, the "ice man" and his earthly possessions continue to reveal much about how humans lived five millennia ago, shattering many previous theories in the process.

That startling Neolithic discovery made on September 19, 1991, on the Similaun Glacier reveals a lot about present-day regionalism and nationalistic sentiments. Ötzi (named for the Ötz Valley Alps where he died) immediately became the focus of a dispute between Austria and Italy.

One of the first concerns was which country had jurisdiction over the find. The bureaucratic custody battle continued, even after a binational survey team confirmed that Ötzi's remains had indeed been found on the Italian side of the bor-

der. In the meantime, Ötzi remained an Austrian resident—in a freezer at the University of Innsbruck. Finally, in 1998, with an armed military escort, the ice man was moved to his new Italian home in a $10 million museum built just for him.

Although the two countries eventually managed to reach an agreement, the process was complicated by several historical factors. One is the fact that the province of South Tyrol (Bolzano in Italian) is an autonomous region within Italy. Tyrol itself has long had an independent, strongly patriotic attitude—its citizens thinking of themselves more as Tyroleans (*Tiroler*) than Austrians.

As recently as the early 1960s, South Tyrolean activists were convicted of terrorist acts in an effort to take South Tyrol back from Italy and reunite it with North Tyrol (Nordtirol) and East Tyrol (Osttirol). Following World War I, the Treaty of Saint Germain ceded South Tyrol to Italy in 1919, despite a German-speaking majority in the region. Almost a century earlier, Andreas Hofer (1767–1810) became a Tyrolean martyr after Napoleon took him prisoner and ordered his execution after Hofer's success in battles against Bavarian and Italo-French forces. Today the "*Andreas-Hofer-Lied*" is the Tyrolean anthem.

Related Web links: provincia.bz.it—see *Museums* for "Der Mann aus dem Eis" Museum in Bolzano (E, G); panorama-innsbruck.at—see *The Hofer Legend* for information on Andreas Hofer (E, G)

Berlin Bleibt Berlin: Berlin Will Always Be Berlin

Berlin stands under the sign of the pickax. In every nook and cranny of downtown, clouds of dust, ramparts of wheelbarrows, and placard-covered construction-site barricades proclaim that one structure is disappearing from the spot to make room for another. It is a never-ending process of rise and fall in modern Berlin. One could even speak of a demolition mania, were this tearing down not far removed from a vandalism that only destroys, and if it did not serve to replace the old with new towering buildings of greater luxury and usefulness through the more efficient use of space.

—BERLINER MORGENPOST

Although it sounds like a commentary about the German capital today, the newspaper excerpt quoted here first appeared in print on November 1, 1906. Almost 100 years after it was written, the only thing needed to make this observation truly contemporary is to replace "pickax" with "bulldozer" and "wheelbarrows" with "construction cranes." Today's Berlin is one huge construction site.

Berlin has always been on the go. Since its early days as the Prussian capital, through its postwar division, and up to its renewed status as Germany's governmental center, Berlin has had an interesting and unique history. Even as a divided city, Berlin was a dynamic place, and few cities can claim a bigger role in modern world history. Today the German metropolis is once again taking on a truly metropolitan character befitting the largest city in the European Union's most populous country. In the 21st century, Berlin has the potential to rival other European capitals.

Not that the city is without any drawbacks. In a metropolitan beauty contest, Berlin would lose to most of its European competition. In many ways, Berlin is more a provincial gathering of small towns than a true metropolis. But then, that is also part of the city's charm.

Related Web links: **berlin.de**—official Berlin site (E, G); **berliner-morgenpost.de**—*Berliner Morgenpost*, newspaper online (G)

A Berlin Time Line

ca. 1200	Two trade settlements, Cölln and Berlin, arise on the banks of the Spree.
1432	Berlin and Cölln become one city: Berlin.
1806	Napoleon occupies Berlin for two-years.
1871	Berlin becomes the capital of the German Reich.
1945	The city is devastated by war and divided in two.
1948–49	Berlin Airlift takes place.
1961	The Berlin Wall is erected.
1989	Fall of the Berlin Wall; Germany is reunited.
1991	Berlin becomes the capital of reunified Germany.
1999	The renovated Reichstag is reopened.

Berlin's historical center and the Friedrichstraße Station were formerly in East Berlin.

The Alps (*Die Alpen*)

The mountains known as the Alps (*die Alpen*) covers four German-speaking countries and stretches across one-quarter of the earth from southeastern France all the way to Vienna. Its snowcapped peaks are sprinkled throughout the German-speaking countries of Austria, Germany, Liechtenstein, and Switzerland. The so-called Alpine Arc forms an 868-mile semicircle from Italy's Gulf of Genoa up through the German-speaking region where Italy and Austria border on each other (the Trentino-Alto Adige region in Italian, the province of Südtirol in German, Bolzano in Italian) and on across into Austria. The Alps are so long and varied that they are usually divided geographically into three sections: the Western, Central, and Eastern Alps. Geologists, however, tend to view the Alps as comprising two main sections divided by the so-called Rhine line, a north-south demarcation that runs through Lake Constance (Bodensee) down across the Septimer Pass just southwest of St. Moritz in Switzerland.

Western Europe's highest peaks are all found in the Alps, most of them in Switzerland. Although it is more famous, the Swiss-Italian Matterhorn tops out at only 14,690 feet, while Monte Rosa (15,203 feet), the Dom (14,911 feet), and the Liskamm (14,852 feet, in Italy and Switzerland) all are higher. The highest Alpine peak is Mont Blanc (15,771 feet), on the French-Italian border. Germany's highest peak is Die Zugspitze, at 9,720 feet.

Of course, the Alps long ago gained fame as the prime location for winter sports, especially downhill skiing (*Abfahrts-lauf*)—which was largely invented in the Austrian Alps and is also known as Alpine skiing, *alpiner Skisport*. (Cross-country skiing, *Langlauf*, comes from Scandinavia.) The Alps are dotted with famous ski resorts in every German-speaking country. Zermatt, situated at the base of the Matterhorn, is a legendary Swiss resort boasting the longest ski season in the Alps. Many Austrians and Swiss learn to ski about the same time they learn to walk.

The Alps are also a favorite for hikers, climbers, and *Sommerfrischler* (loosely, "summer fresh-air freaks"). A vast network of *Wanderwege*, or hiking trails, crisscrosses the Alps and the four countries they cover. There are 10 designated *Weitwanderwege* (long-distance trails) found in the Austrian Alps alone, from the Nordalpenweg (Rust am Neusiedlersee–Semmering–Kufstein–Bregenz on Lake Constance) to the Rupertiweg (Bärnstein in the Böhmerwald–Salzburg–Königsee–Naßfeld in the Corinthian Alps). Even longer European trails run in both north-south and east-west routes across the continent, including the Alps.

Related Web links: alpseurope.org—The Alps (E); http://**homepage.boku.ac.at/h505ta /weit.htm**—Weitwanderwege for hiking trails in Austria and Europe (G)

Killer Drafts and *Kreislaufstörung*: Germans and Their Favorite Ailments

Certain nationalities seem to fall prey to particular aches and pains. The French complain about their livers, Americans about their rheumatism, and Germans . . . well, Germans have a unique ailment of which few non-Germans have ever heard.

Since the Germans long ago perfected the art of worrying in general, it should come as no shock that what they most often worry about is their health. And when they worry about their health, the most frequent concern is something called *Kreislaufstörung*, an amazing collection of circulatory ailments that can range from a headache to a heart attack. Indeed, it is difficult to find an illness that a German wouldn't classify as a *Kreislaufstörung* (circulation problem).

It is, in fact, this national preoccupation with *Kreislaufstörung* that in part led to Germany's spa tradition, a health-craze phenomenon that is rarely surpassed in any other culture. Taking the "cure" or the "waters" (*eine Kur machen*) is not only frequently prescribed by German doctors but also covered by German health insurance. The German language created the word *Kurort* (spa resort) just for places like Baden-Baden (spa-spa or bath-bath) that live off the German compulsion to take the waters. Of course, spas help with other non-*Kreislaufstörung* aches and pains (if there is such a thing), and Germans feel it is their right and duty to visit a spa at least once a year.

There is one more important German health concern of which any foreigner should be aware. The expression *es zieht* (there's a draft) will echo in your brain

should you ever have the temerity to even slightly crack open a window on a hot summer day while on a moving train or in an automobile going more than five miles per hour. Germans and some other Europeans consider even the slightest breeze from an open window to be fatal! To the German mind, such a killer draft will surely lead to your demise from pneumonia or some other serious draft-related ailment. On certain German and Austrian streetcars, there are even signs admonishing passengers to not leave windows open. The whole thing gives an entirely new meaning to "avoiding the draft"! It makes one wonder just how Germany could possibly be the birthplace of the motorcar.

Kurort: Literally, "cure place," *Kurort* is an official designation for an area or resort specializing in the natural health remedies of mineral baths. German health insurance (*Krankenkasse*) covers these treatments. These places levy a special *Kurtaxe* on patients taking the cure. The term *Heilbad* or *Bad* (health spa, bath) is also an official one. Towns with *Bad* in their names are often also *Kurorte*.

Related Web links: http://baden-baden.de—
Baden-Baden (E, G); rathen.de (G);
badabbach.de (G); badgriesbach.de (G);
badsassendorf-online.de (G)

Smoker's Paradise?

For all their fanaticism about fresh air and healthy foods, Germans, Austrians, the Swiss, and Europeans in general are incredibly blasé about smoking. Although the smoking rate in Germany is only somewhat higher than in antismoking bastions such as the United States, it sometimes seems as if every living adult German smokes! That is because Germany has few smoking restrictions in public places, the workplace, and even restaurants.

It's not that Germany's 20 million smokers haven't been told about the evidence concerning the increased health risks of smoking. Printed warnings about the dangers of smoking, similar to those in other countries, must appear in print ads and on every pack of cigarettes sold in the country. Lately, members of the long-protected German species known as *Raucher* (smokers) have begun to face a few limited restrictions. Even passive smoke, for many years a nonissue in Germany, has come under attack, although certainly not to the same degree as in the United States. (Most Germans familiar with the strong antismoking attitudes in the United States think Americans are fanatics about the issue.)

There have been some other restrictions concerning smoking in Germany, but these qualify primarily as preventive measures. Tobacco ads on German television have been verboten since 1978. European trains have long had smoking and nonsmoking cars. Even Lufthansa, a German airline, has smoking and nonsmoking seating. Although they are now less rare, if you ask for the nonsmoking section in a typical German restaurant and you'll suddenly feel as if you're from another planet.

Designated smoking and nonsmoking sections in the workplace are also rare. Smoking in public places is regarded by most Germans as a basic constitutional right. When neighboring France introduced antismoking laws in 1992, German smokers indulged in a bit of schadenfreude. But their days of gloating may be numbered.

According to the Germans' own statistics, about 70,000 Germans die each year of smoking-related diseases. So, back in the mid-1990s when a coalition of some 100 members of the Bundestag drafted a resolution to introduce legislation restricting smoking in public, Germany's tiny antismoking group Nichtraucher-Initiative Deutschland (NID), as well as cancer and medical societies, lent their support. Karsten Vilmar, head of the German Doctors Association, even pushed for a special "health tax" (*Gesundheitssteuer*) on cigarettes. Predictably, the German tobacco lobby weighed in heavily against any effort to clamp down on smokers. The Federal Association for the Cigarette Industry claimed that not only would the one-third of Germans who smoked object, but also that 70 to 80 percent of all Germans would not stand for legal restrictions on smoking in public. The tobacco lobby had no cause for worry then, but the antismoking NID is still around.

Related Web link: ni-d.de—Nichtraucher-Initiative Deutschland (NID) (G)

Your Friendly *Apotheker*

One of the strengths of the German health-care system is the modest institution known as the *Apotheke*, the local pharmacy. If you are used to the convenience of buying nonprescription drugs and health-care products "over the counter" at any supermarket or drugstore, the first time you try to do this in Austria, Germany, or Switzerland will likely be a frustrating experience. It can't be done.

It seems odd that in the land where aspirin was invented it is difficult to obtain any. Even if you just want some aspirin, cold medicine, or other nonprescription painkiller, you will have to go to an *Apotheke* (apothecary shop). Just look for a big red "A" for *Apotheke*. Once there, you'll find that the German version of a pharmacy offers certain compensations for any loss of drug-buying freedom. The *Apotheker* serves as a combination doctor and pharmacist, filling a role that differs to a significant degree from the American counterpart.

A *Drogerie*, despite its name, isn't a drugstore. A *Drogerie* doesn't sell drugs or medicines. A German "drugstore" is more of a minimart for beauty products, toiletries, and detergents, but no medicines. Even in the *Apotheke*, you can't simply pick out a box of aspirin and pay for it. All the *Arzneimittel* (medications), prescription or not, are located behind the counter or in the back room. You may have to ask the *Apotheker* for something to treat a headache (*Kopfweh*). This person will then ask a few questions about what the problem could be and will soon come up with some appropriate *Medikament*. It's unlikely to be plain aspirin unless you insist on aspirin.

During nights and holidays, designated *Apotheken* stay open. Your doctor (*Arzt*) will usually tell you which pharmacy is open, but if you don't know, you can go to any nearby *Apotheke* and read the sign in the door that tells you the address of the one that is open that day. This information is also published daily in the local newspaper and sometimes online.

Your *Apotheker* can sometimes save you a trip to the doctor by giving you pharmacological advice. If you do not speak German, you should still do fine: many pharmacists in German Europe speak English, or you can use sign language and pointing to indicate your particular problem if you don't have a German-speaking friend to help you. If you have a written prescription (*Rezept*) from a doctor, there is little difficulty.

> ### Prescription Refills
> If you require a certain medication and will be in German Europe for some time, it is advisable to take along a supply of the medication and a prescription for refills. A drug may be known in your home country by a different name from that in Europe. Some medications may not even be available at all in the other country due to different regulations. A sample may help determine the equivalent drug. The same advice is valid for eyeglasses and contact lens prescriptions.

The Captain from Köpenick: The Cobbler's New Clothes

In 1906, Wilhelm Voigt was a 57-year-old ex-con and ex-cobbler who would soon be known as the "Captain from Köpenick" (*der Hauptmann von Köpenick*). Following his release from prison, Voigt was caught in a catch-22 situation: in order to get a job, he needed a passport, but without a job he couldn't get a passport. Several attempts to secure a passport from the Prussian bureaucracy had not only proved fruitless but also led to his expulsion from Berlin.

In desperation, Voigt managed to procure a discarded Prussian captain's uniform from a secondhand shop. On October 16, 1906, he donned the uniform and assumed the role of captain (*Hauptmann*). He then commandeered a detail of soldiers, marched them to the town of Köpenick (now a district of Berlin), occupied the city hall, used forged orders to have the mayor arrested, and, to top it all off, made off with a strongbox containing about 4,000 marks from the town treasury. In a twist of irony, Voigt discovered that there was no passport office in the city hall.

After his own arrest and a two-day trial, Voigt was sentenced to four years in prison. In the meantime, the scoundrel shoemaker had become a folk hero in Prussia. Even Kaiser Wilhelm II was sympathetic enough to pardon Voigt before he had served half of his prison term.

The German playwright Carl Zuckmayer helped ensure that the Köpenick legend would live on. His *deutsches Märchen* (German fairy tale) dramatization of the event, starring some of the best actors of the time, had its premiere in Berlin on March 5, 1931. The Voigt story was also made into a German film in 1956, starring Heinz Rühmann.

Voigt's *Köpenickiade* (Köpenick escapade) cast both the Prussian bureaucracy and Prussian respect for the uniform over the man in a bad light. The "cobbler's new clothes" exposed the tendency of Germans to follow authority. Few true stories better illustrate the German maxim *Kleider machen Leute* (Clothes make the man). It was not only the Berliners who took a certain delight in Voigt's successful charade; his exposure of the stupidity of blind obedience and appearance over substance was a story that spread across Prussia and much of the rest of the world in 1906.

The real-life fairy tale had a relatively happy ending. Voigt, who had spent about 30 years of his life in prison, basked briefly in his Köpenick celebrity, even visiting the United States in 1910. He made enough money to manage a new start as a cobbler in Luxembourg, where he died in 1922.

In 1998, a life-size sculpture of Wilhelm Voigt, alias "Captain from Köpenick," was dedicated in the Berlin-Köpenick city hall. The long-overdue memorial, created by the Armenian artist Spartak Babajan, was installed in a ceremony that included a reenactment of the *Köpenickiade.*

Related Web link: wild-east.de/berlin/koepenick /rathaus.html—Köpenick-Rathaus, photo of the city hall in the distance and brief information about the Köpenick story (G)

German Women: Yesterday and Today

There is no disputing that Germany has been and remains a male-dominated society. Even in the Bundesrepublik (Federal Republic of Germany) of the 21st century, a current list of the 100 most influential Germans would contain very few women. (Just such a recently published list featured only four.) A list of famous Germans in history displays an even lower percentage of females, but that is hardly just a German phenomenon.

Nevertheless, a few notable women have overcome the German "triple K" stereotype that relegated females to *Kinder, Kirche, Küche* (children, church, kitchen). The emergence of the "modern German woman" of recent times dates back to the *Trümmerfrauen* of the 1940s, the tough, hardworking, no-nonsense women who salvaged a war-devastated Germany by clearing the rubble, tending to people who were wounded, and helping Germany rebuild itself. Many of those women and their daughters went on to become influential in fields as diverse as politics, fashion, sports, cinema, and the arts:

- **Doris Dörrie** (1955–) Film director, writer
- **Stefanie Maria Graf** (1969–) Tennis champion
- **Maria Goeppert Mayer** (1906–72) Winner of Nobel Prize in physics, 1963
- **Anne-Sophie Mutter** (1963–) Internationally acclaimed violinist
- **Jil Sander** (1943–) Fashion designer
- **Alice Schwarzer** (1942–) German women's movement leader, publisher of *Emma* magazine

- **Elisabeth Schwarzhaupt** (1901–86) First female German cabinet member (health minister, 1961–66)
- **Heide Simonis** (1943–) First female governor of a German *Bundesland* (Schleswig-Holstein)
- **Rita Süssmuth** (1937–) President of Bundestag, 1988–98

Earlier in Germany, there were also women whose achievements have earned them a spot on the list of famous women of history. It is ironic that one of the most notable, Leni Riefenstahl, was a product of the Nazi era, when women were typically viewed as bearers and raisers of children. Some historical Germanic females:

- **Lise Meitner** (1878–1968) Austrian nuclear physicist (fission)
- **Leni Riefenstahl** (1902–) Film director (*Olympia*), still photographer
- **Clara Schumann** (1819–96) Pianist, composer

By the way, German women got the right to vote in 1918, two years before American women.

Related Web links: ipts.de/women/frauen.htm—for Project Women links (E, G); ipts.de/women/berhmted.htm—for Berühmte deutsche Frauen, famous German women (G); politea-project.de—More German women of note (G)

Five Decades of Democracy

Turning 50 was a time for reflection in the Bundesrepublik. Just exactly when they should celebrate their country's 50th birthday was no certainty for Germany's citizens (*Bundesbürger*). The Federal Republic of Germany came into existence in a series of events that began with the introduction of the new Deutsche Mark currency in July 1948 and ended with the first session of the German lower house (Bundestag) and the formation of the country's first federal government (Bundesregierung) in September 1949. (In the eastern part of the country, another German republic, the Deutsche Demokratische Republik, had also been formed in 1949. If reunification had not ended its existence in 1990, the German Democratic Republic also would have celebrated its 50th birthday in 1999.)

But picking a specific date was the least of the problems connected with the German birthday celebration. As with almost anything German, the country's past colored even how it would commemorate its birthday. The horrors and excesses of the National Socialist (Nazi) era — which ended around the same time that the new Bundesrepublik began — gave "nationalism" a bad name in modern Germany. Although the radical right, skinheads, and neo-Nazis in today's Germany too often make the headlines, the vast majority of Germans are extremely uncomfortable with anything that smacks of nationalistic excess. German flag-waving is confined to team banners in soccer stadiums. If you look, it's difficult to even *find* a flag to wave. Not even many government buildings display the national flag.

There is no German equivalent of the American Independence Day celebration. (Firecrackers *are* heard in Germany, but mostly on New Year's Eve, *Silvester!*) How do you celebrate a nation's birthday when open patriotism is considered to be in poor taste? How do you celebrate a birthday when the country actually has several dates from which to choose?

Few Germans even know the date of their country's founding. It was on May 23, 1949, that the Federal Republic of Germany's Basic Law (*Grundgesetz*), or constitution, went into effect. But May 23 has never been a German holiday. How about November 9, the date of the opening of the Berlin Wall in 1989? No, too much heavy baggage from the Nazi *Kristallnacht* anti-Jewish pogroms that began on the night of November 9, 1938. So, German Unity Day (*Tag der deutschen Einheit*) is now celebrated on October 3, the official date of German reunification in 1990.

Related Web links: bundestag.de—German parliament (E, G); **bundesregierung.de**—German government (E, G)

The new glass dome atop the Reichstag is open to the public.

Trautes Heim, Glück Allein (Your Home Is Your Castle)

There's one area where Europe's largest nation has a lot of catching up to do. Germany has one of the lowest rates of home ownership in all of Europe. Spain, at the top, can boast 85 percent of Spaniards living in a house or apartment they own. Americans and Britons have a respectable rate of homeownership at 67 and 68 percent, respectively. Just to Germany's south, about 55 percent of Austrians own their own domiciles, still higher than the German rate. France, Germany's neighbor to the west, has a rate of 54 percent, just under that of Austria. But only about 42 percent of all Germans are homeowners.

Why does Germany, with Europe's leading economy, rank at the bottom of the homeownership totem pole? There is no one simple answer, but a vital factor is surely the high cost of land and housing. Another is the traditionally high-percentage down payment that German lenders demand, often as much as 50 percent, and shorter loan periods. Rather than the U.S. standard of a 15- or 30-year mortgage (*Hypotheke*) with 10 to 20 percent down, German banks offer 5- or 10-year terms, which makes monthly payments much higher. A 22-year mortgage is considered a long mortgage in Germany.

The cost of buying a home in Germany can vary greatly, depending on where you choose to live. A recent survey of housing costs by Germany's *Focus* magazine reflected a wide range of prices. The price of a typical new attached/row house (*Reihenhaus*) in Germany in 2001 ranged from a high of 525,000 euros ($462,580) in Stuttgart down to a low of 155,000 euros ($136,570) in eastern Berlin (larger cities only; smaller towns are usually cheaper). Germany's housing bargains can be found in the eastern regions of the country, while popular western cities (Berlin, Stuttgart, Munich, Frankfurt am Main) had the highest housing costs. See the chart below for sample price ranges in various German cities.

Average Cost (in euros, 2001) of a typical row house

Berlin (west)	210,000–400,000
Berlin (east)	155,000–270,000
Dresden	160,000–260,000
Frankfurt	265,000–425,000
Hamburg	200,000–375,000
Munich	305,000–500,000
Stuttgart	265,000–525,000

Source: *Focus*, Bulwien AG

Related Web links: A selection of nationwide real estate agents: **immobilien.de** (G), **remax.de** (G), **immowelt.de** (G), **ev-immo.de**—Engels & Völkers (E, G)

Advice on buying real estate in Germany: **real-estate-european-union.com/english/germany.html** (E), **allgrund.com/realestate** (E)

In der Küche: Everything but the Kitchen Sink?

The German word *Küche* means both "kitchen" and "cuisine." *Deutsche Küche* (German cuisine) is created in a German *Küche*. The kitchen in a German, Austrian, or Swiss home is usually smaller and more compact than its North American counterpart—not only because European homes and apartments themselves tend to be smaller, but also because European kitchen appliances are usually smaller and more economical. A typical German (or European) refrigerator (*Kühlschrank*) is about half the size of an American one. It therefore holds about half as much and uses half the energy. This is possible because traditionally, German homemakers shopped daily for groceries and therefore required less refrigerator space. Over the last two decades or so, though, Germans have been reducing the frequency of their grocery shopping to once or twice a week, making a larger *Kühlschrank* necessary. Of course, full-size refrigerators are available for those who prefer them and can afford to pay the higher purchase cost and the extra electricity charges.

If you are planning to buy or rent a German apartment, be aware that it may come with a "bare" kitchen. *Bare* is indeed the right word. Your new kitchen may be nothing more than four bare walls with roughed-in plumbing and electrical connections—even the kitchen sink may be missing! There are true stories of unsuspecting Americans moving into a new German apartment, only to end up doing the dishes in the bathroom sink (by candlelight) until they could install a new sink in the kitchen (and a bathroom light).

Once you have a kitchen sink (*der Ausguß, das Spülbecken*) in Germany, it will be missing something that is standard equipment in North American kitchens: an in-sink garbage disposal (*der Müllschlucker, der Küchenabfallzerkleinerer*). For environmental reasons, these devices have been outlawed in Germany since the 1960s. That situation could change, though. Because of advances in sewage treatment, there has been some recent discussion about possibly allowing garbage disposals to appear in German kitchens.

Related Web links: Kitchen appliance manufacturers: **aeg.hausgeraete.de**—*AEG* (G); **miele.de**—Miele (G), **bosch-hausgeraete.de**—Bosch, see *Products/Produkte* (E, G)
  Kitchen appliance retailer: **moebelcenter woessner.de**—Möbel (G)

Washing Machines Versus *Waschmaschinen*: Which Clean Better?

Boil (*kochen*) or bleach (*bleichen*)? Top loader (*Toplader*) or front loader (*Frontlader*)? Short or long wash cycles? The debate about the alleged superiority of German/European washing machines versus American ones can reach a surprising intensity. German machines tend to be front loaders, while the American version is usually a top loader. Germans maintain that their washing machines clean far better than the North American equivalent.

Actually, independent comparisons indicate that both—whether top loader, front loader, European, or American—clean equally well. The real differences lie more in the area of economy (and ecology) and two distinct wash philosophies. Although Germans can buy top-loading machines, the great majority of European washing machines are front loading. (In North America, the situation is reversed.) Front-loading machines usually cost several hundred dollars more than top loaders, but they make up for this by being quieter and much more economical to run, using less water and energy.

German appliance maker Miele manufactured its first wooden tub muscle-powered agitator washing machine in 1901. Since then, Miele and other brands, with names such as AEG, Bauknecht, and Bosch, have gone on to be innovators in the field. The electricity and water consumption of European washing machines has been cut in half over the past 15 years, and there is now an EU (European Union) standard for all such appliances.

A North American using a German *Waschmaschine* (also called a *Waschau-*

tomat) for the first time is in for several surprises. One of the biggest is the fact that a German machine often has a washing cycle as long as two hours! One Bosch machine has a wash program of 125 minutes but uses only 45 liters (11.8 gallons) of water per wash cycle. Compare that with one of the most economical U.S. front-loading models, which uses 103 liters (27 gallons) of water, or more than twice as much.

German *Waschmaschinen* also preheat the water to very hot temperatures (60 degrees centigrade, 140 degrees Fahrenheit), while U.S. machines use hot water from the water heater at 100 to 120 degrees Fahrenheit. Higher wash temperatures mean a German hausfrau has to use less bleach. Whites and cottons are usually washed at temperatures close to boiling (95 degrees centigrade, *Kochwäsche*). This, claim the environmentally conscious Germans, leads to less pollution, and since the washer heats only the water it needs, there is less energy consumption as well.

German machines also have high spin speeds (up to 1,600 revolutions per minute), which are more efficient in wringing most of the water out of the wash. Although most Germans hang the wash out to dry, those using a dryer use less energy because the clothes are better prepared for drying.

Related Web links: aeg.hausgeraete.de—AEG (G); bosch.de—Bosch (E, G); miele.de—Miele (E, G); bauknecht.de—Bauknecht (G)

The Garbage Police

Few countries in the world are as picky about their waste as Germany is. Many German communities, large and small, even have special websites to explain all the variations and requirements for garbage day.

In Germany, you don't just toss anything at random into the garbage pail or wastebasket. Almost every community has strict rules about *Mülltrennung*, or waste separation, and garbage collectors are strict about those rules. If you have mixed your glass waste with the *Bioabfälle* (biodegradable waste), neither will get picked up. Certain waste categories are collected less or more frequently, and there are separate containers for each one, designated by labels and differing colors.

The *Biotonne* (bio can) is strictly for biodegradable waste. According to the online garbage guidelines for the city of Heilbronn, biodegradable waste makes up about 40 percent of household waste. Such waste is now composted by the waste authority, and a separate *Biotonne* is required. What can't go into the bio can? ". . . disposable diapers, sanitary napkins, fluid food waste, vacuum bags, ashes, cigarette butts, sweepings, plastic bags, drink cartons, textiles, leather, wool, layered paper, brochures." Only food leftovers, eggshells, hair, paper napkins, grass cuttings, and the like are allowed. During most of the year, *Biotonne* pickup is every 14 days. Only during the months of June, July, and August is biodegradable waste collected weekly.

The "Yellow Sack" (*Gelber Sack*) or yellow container is intended for disposal of packaging materials, including foil, plastic, aluminum cans, and plastic bottles. Used paper, cardboard, and glass do *not* go into the yellow container; they need to be placed in special collection containers for recycling. There are also special rules for the disposal of batteries, household and/or hazardous chemicals, building materials, *das Recyling*, and other categories.

Mannheim's online "*Abfall von A–Z*" ("Waste from A to Z") stresses the avoidance of waste in the first place. It promotes the two Vs: *Vermeiden und Verwerten* (avoid and process). The Mannheim guidelines say that you should think about garbage when you shop: "Therefore you should avoid items with too much packaging as well as throwaway products." The directive then goes on to give half a dozen suggestions for avoiding waste. One of these tips is something that many Germans do anyway: take along your own shopping bag and avoid plastic disposable bags (for which most German stores charge extra).

Related Web link: hnonline.de/service/muell—
Heilbronn Online, *Abfallratgeber* (waste adviser) (G)

Kehrwoche: Your Turn to Sweep!

Germans are known for their obsession with cleanliness (*Sauberkeit*) and order (*Ordnung*). In order to maintain these German virtues in many apartment buildings, the Germans have created the dreaded system called *Kehrwoche,* or "sweep week."

Kehrwoche can involve much more than a bit of sweeping. The whole idea is to share the chores of keeping the common areas—stairways, walkways, vestibules, and such—clean and tidy. And safe, as in winter, when an icy sidewalk could become a problem, or in the fall, when wet, slippery leaves can pose a hazard.

The system varies from place to place, but generally you will spot a so-called *Kehrwoche-Kalender*—a schedule of when which residents have the *Kehrwoche* responsibilities. Sometimes the landlord sends out a printed notice to all tenants in the building, while other apartment houses place a "*Kehrwoche*" sign next to the door of the designated apartment for that week. In any event, tenants who do not carry out their cleaning duties, or don't do them to the degree expected, can be subject to withering looks or outright snide comments.

Just what happens during *Kehrwoche*? If this is your first time dealing with "sweep week," it's a good idea to observe what your fellow apartment dwellers do. Most apartments have a list of duties, and in most cases your *Kehrwoche* obligations are even stipulated as part of your rental contract. Except during the winter season, usually the main thing is to sweep and mop the stairs, landings, entryway, and other common areas. In winter, the sidewalks should be shoveled and sanded. (Salt is usually frowned on or even illegal. Shoveling snow on walks is sometimes optional.)

Knowing all this, you may wish to consider an apartment building with contracted cleaning services. Larger apartment complexes usually do not have *Kehrwoche*. The minus side is that such apartments may be more expensive than those where the tenants do the dirty work. Before you sign that rental contract, make sure you know whether you'll have janitorial duties or not!

Invasion of the *Gartenzwerge*

Germans have always loved their *Garten-zwerge*, the colorful, chubby-cheeked ceramic statues that adorn many of the country's front yards and gardens. Despite being viewed by many Germans as *kitschig* (tacky, kitschy) and the equivalent of artificial pink flamingos, the garden gnome has proved to be an enduring German phenomenon that thrives on both the German love of gardening and the need to stake out territory. It is said that the garden dwarf actually came to Germany centuries ago via a circuitous route from Turkey via Italy. The original 14th-century Turkish versions were stone statuettes of African pygmy slaves who worked in Turkish mines.

A typical German ceramic lederhosen-clad little person costs about 50 euros (around $44) or more. (There are more than 300 different gnome designs, some of them copyrighted.) Most of the German *Gartenzwerge* come from the southern state of Bavaria (Bayern), but in recent years, German gnome makers have been facing a threat to their existence: cheap Polish knockoffs. Polish gnome plastic look-alikes sell for as little as a 10th of the cost of the German originals. In the Polish town of Nowa Sol alone, 40 factories crank out a constant supply of garden gnome doppelgängers.

To counter the Polish invasion, the Germans began making their own plastic statuettes, while also pointing out that the Polish versions owed their colorful appearance to dangerous lead-based paint and were otherwise inferior to the German product. Meanwhile, their rivals in Poland were shamelessly cloning the Germans'

gnome designs, copyrighted or not. Fearing for their survival, two German gnome producers filed suit in May 1994 against the Polish copycats.

For the Bavarian gnome producer Zeho, it was too little, too late. Zeho went out of business in 1999 after the Poles had stolen many of its designs. Although the lawsuit resulted in crackdowns on Polish imports and even gnome quotas for returning German tourists at the Polish-German border, the Poles have proved wily in avoiding copyright infringements. While some German gnome makers have been forced to survive by avoiding plastic and catering to the more upscale ceramic market, German gnome production has fallen. German gnome lovers just can't resist the bargain prices of the Polish-made garden gnomes. Now the Germans can only hope that Poland will soon enter the European Union and will then compete on a more level playing field. After all, they like to point out, the Poles sell almost none of their gnome production in Poland. Most Polish gnomes emigrate to Germany, while the rest find homes in other countries, including the United States.

Related Web link: zwergen-power.de—
a German gnome manufacturer and retailer (G)

Doors and Locks

German doors and locks are an indication of the German obsession with privacy. Doors, exterior or interior, are sturdy, well-crafted barriers to intrusion. In homes and offices, doors are numerous and more likely to be closed than open. An open-door policy is a rarity in Germany.

To keep them closed, German locks are made to standards that are equal to or better than the doors they secure. They are an imposing construction of tumblers, pins, shafts, bolts, and double-locking mechanisms with keys to match—a locksmith's dream and a burglar's nightmare. Outside door locks are almost always double-locked affairs that require a special course just to learn how to use them.

The Romans invented metal locks, but German locksmiths, particularly in Nürnberg in the Middle Ages, are credited with improving the devices. More modern improvements, including the American Yale lock and the more recent Swiss Kaba lock, are refinements of the ancient Egyptian wooden pin-tumbler lock. The Kaba lock features a smooth-sided key with dimplelike depressions, unlike most keys, which usually have serrated, grooved sides.

Increasingly, German hotels, especially upscale ones, are using computer-coded locks with magnetic key cards.

Along with substantial fences, thick hedges, roll-down metal shutters (*Rolladen*), iron gates, double-paned windows, and other spatially defining constructions, the German door commands respect and maintains the privacy of its owner. Behind that closed door, Germans can count on comfort and privacy. It serves both to keep things out (noise, people) and to keep things in (warmth, a secure feeling).

Traditionally, a German door kept in the warmth when only one room of the house was heated in winter. Today, despite central heating, every room, even in a small apartment, has a door with lock and key. In an office building, doors serve to keep out the noise from corridors and fellow workers.

All those doors help serve to separate and define Germanic space. Like a medieval castle, a German home or office has clearly defined compartments. Many Germans are confused by modern open-space offices that lack those solid divisions.

Related Web links: fsb.de—FSB-Klinken, a German maker of door latches (E, G); **hewi.de**—HEWI, a German maker of door latches (G)

Crime: A Few Surprises

As in most other countries, the German crime rate varies from place to place. In 1998, the dubious honor of being Germany's most crime-ridden city went to Frankfurt am Main. Germany's banking and financial capital in the state of Hesse recorded 19,128 crimes per 100,000, a figure that far exceeded even the 11,897-per-100,000 rate of Washington, D.C., a city known for its relatively high crime level.

On the opposite end of the German crime spectrum was the city of Solingen in North Rhine-Westphalia. The good citizens of Solingen, with a crime rate of 5,097 per 100,000 population, were almost four times safer than those living in Frankfurt. Hagen, in the same state, with 7,057 crimes per 100,000, was rated the safest of all German cities with more than 200,000 in population.

It may be a surprise to learn that Hagen's "low" crime rate is higher than the average in the United States. The overall crime index in the United States for 1998 was only 5,079 (about the same as Solingen, Germany's safest town). Germany's overall rate was 7,869 per 100,000. On the surface, that means that Germany's crime rate was 35.5 percent higher. In fact, if only property crimes are counted, many European countries, including England, the Netherlands, and Sweden, have a higher crime rate than that of the United States. In that regard, it is only fair to point out that the percentage of crimes not reported to the police in Germany is lower than in the United States.

However, in a comparison of violent crime, Germany and the rest of Europe come out clear winners. Berlin, the "leading" German metropolis for murder, had a total of 96 murders in 1998 (including nonnegligent manslaughter), a rate of 2.8 per 100,000. That same year, Chicago, with only a slightly lower population, had 694 murders, closer to 25 per 100,000, or more than nine times the Berlin rate. Los Angeles, Berlin's sister city, with about the same population, had a murder rate of 20.3 in 1996. The average U.S. murder rate in 1997 was 6.8 per 100,000, while Germany's rate was 1.4 per 100,000. These statistics are even more remarkable when one notes that Germany has no death penalty.

Sources: BKA *Polizeiliche Kriminalstatistik*; FBI Uniform Crime Reports

Related Web links: bka.de—*Bundeskriminalamt* (G); **fbi.gov/ucr/ucr.htm**—FBI Uniform Crime Reports, for U.S. figures (E)

The *Länder* Police Forces

German law and the German law enforcement system have evolved over the centuries, going back to ancient Germanic tribal customs, Roman influences, feudal law, and later the Napoleonic Code. The modern German police force is also a product of the Allied effort to restore democracy to Germany after World War II. Another significant factor was the total rejection of the all-powerful Nazi police state that ruled Germany until the end of the war in 1945. The result of all these influences is a largely decentralized system under which, with only a few exceptions, each of Germany's 16 *Bundesländer*, or federal states, is responsible for administering law enforcement.

In their familiar forest green jackets, brown pants, and green-and-white cars, German police officers look more centralized and standardized than they actually are. While their uniforms and vehicles may look the same, there are 16 different *Land* police forces across Germany handling everyday law enforcement matters, from giving out speeding tickets to tracking down murderers. Larger cities may also have their own municipal police forces; three large German cities are also states: Berlin, Bremen, and Hamburg.

Although there are two important exceptions to Germany's decentralized police system, the federal BKA (the Bundeskriminalamt, Germany's FBI) and the BGS (Bundesgrenzschutz, the federal border guard), those two agencies are limited to specific areas of law enforcement. The major responsibility for enforcing the law in Germany falls to the *Länder*, the states.

Almost all of the 16 *Länderpolizeien* have a website with information about their services and how to contact them. (The Germany-wide emergency police phone number is 110. Fire is 112.) In any larger German city, a local *Polizeipräsidium* (police station) can be found in various neighborhoods or sections of the city. It is usually here that you must register as a resident (*anmelden*) when you move in.

Related Web links: polizei-online.de—an unofficial information site with links to all of the German police agencies that are online (G); polizei.bayern.de—Polizei Bayern, Bavarian police force (G); polizei.berlin.de—Berlin police force (E, G) (Most of the German *Länderpolizeien* have similarly addressed sites.)

Municipal police forces can be found under each state, as with Düsseldorf, cited here, in the Land of Nordrhein-Westfalen. A sampling: justiz.bayern.de—*Bayerisches Staatsministerium der Justiz,* Bavaria's ministry of justice (G); polizei.nrw.de/duesseldorf—the Düsseldorf police website (E, G); polizei.gv.at—links and information for Austria's police (G); polizei.ch—links and information for the Swiss police (G)

Die Polizei: BKA and BGS

As noted, the German law enforcement system is a largely decentralized system, with most police powers delegated to Germany's 16 *Bundesländer*. The two main exceptions to this decentralized model are the Bundeskriminalant (BKA), headquartered in Wiesbaden, and the Bundesgrenzschutz (BGS), a federally run police force under the German ministry of the interior (Innenministerium).

While perhaps not as glamorous or well known as the FBI in the United States, the BKA plays a similar role in German law enforcement. It is the BKA that maintains Germany's central police archives, supports local law enforcement efforts, coordinates activities at the international level (Interpol, Europol, and foreign police authorities), protects officials in the German federal government, investigates certain types of crimes (international terrorism, threats against federal officials, and so forth), and is responsible for witness protection.

The BKA trains its own agents and officials in a three-year program at the Fachhochschule des Bundes für öffentliche Verwaltung (Federal Academy for Public Administration) and also helps train other police personnel, especially in the area of criminal technology (DNA analysis, forensics).

The BKA was established in 1951 by the so-called *BKA-Gesetz* (BKA law). Since then, its role in German law enforcement has steadily increased. In 1955, there were only 500 BKA employees. By 1998, there were 4,300, of whom some 2,000 were BKA agents. Over the years, revisions in the law have created new BKA units or divisions to deal with illegal drugs, weapons violations, and counterfeiting. An antiterrorism unit was created in 1975, and in 1983, the BKA sent its first drug interdiction teams outside of Germany.

The paramilitary BGS, as its name implies, does guard Germany's non–EU borders. But since the organization's establishment in 1951, the armed members of the BGS also guard airports and railways, the offices of the federal president and the federal chancellor, as well as other key federal buildings. The BGS-See is the BGS coast guard unit, with patrol craft and helicopters. The BGS also functions as a reserve force to back up the *Land* police in emergencies or for major turmoil.

The deaths of 11 Israeli hostages, five of their captors, and a German policeman in a failed rescue attempt during the infamous Palestinian terrorist attack at the 1972 Olympics in Munich led to the formation of a special BGS unit known as BGS-9. In 1977, the BGS-9 task force proved its value by rescuing 86 passengers from a hijacked Lufthansa jet in Mogadishu, Somalia.

Related Web links: bka.de—Bundeskriminalamt (BKA) official site (G); **bka.de/pks/pks1999 /summary.html**—BKA, English summary of German crime statistics, 1999 (check for updates) (E); **bundesgrenzschutz.de**— Bundesgrenzschutz official site (G)

German in Germany: What You Don't Know Can Hurt You

Spending time in Germany or any other foreign land without knowing anything about the language of the natives is not only foolish but also frustrating. Beyond the fact that you will be more effective, and life will be more fun and interesting, if you're familiar with the local lingo, there are practical reasons for knowing the language.

For instance, you should be aware that while *Ausgang* means exit, *Notausgang* does *not* mean "not an exit" but rather "emergency exit." Sitting at a *Stammtisch* could get you in trouble if you didn't know that it is a table reserved for regular customers only. *Einstieg* tells you which end of the streetcar to board. A *Sommerschlußverkauf* is a big summer sale that could save you money, while *Hochspannung* is high voltage that could kill you.

Also, as explained in the "Daily Life and Customs" chapter, confusing *du*, *ihr*, and *Sie*, the three German words for *you*, can lead to a social faux pas that could scuttle a business deal or at the very least make your German friends quite uncomfortable. When in doubt, use *Sie*—and learn the language.

Related Web links: german.about.com—German language (E,G); **goethe.de**—The Goethe Institute offers language courses for foreigners, both in Germany and in various other countries around the world (G, E)

False Friends and Imposters

The similarities between English and German can be risky. Many German words can be "false friends"—words that seem to be something they are not. Linguists refer to them as "false cognates" because they appear to be the same as their English relations, but they can mean something altogether different in German. Their misuse can cause problems ranging from mild amusement to extreme embarrassment. English speakers should be aware of the following common German "false friends":

- *aktuell* = up-to-date, current, present ("actual" is *echt* or *wirklich*; "actually" is *eigentlich*)
- *also* = thus, therefore (English "also" is *auch* in German)
- *das Argument* = a reasoned argument or point, usually not a disagreement (*der Streit*)
- *bald* = soon
- *Billion* = trillion (an American "billion" is *eine Milliarde* in German)
- *Box* = speaker for a stereo system; electrical or telecommunications junction box
- *die City* = the downtown city center of a larger town (although it sometimes equals *Stadt* (town)
- *der Dom* = cathedral (a "dome" is *eine Kuppel*)
- *das Etikett* = label, sticker, tag ("etiquette" is *die Etikette* or *Anstandsregeln*)
- *Evergreen* = an old musical standard, a classic popular song (not trees)
- *fast* = almost

- *der Fotograf* = photographer (a "photograph" is *ein Foto*)
- *die Garage* = garage of a house (a garage for repairs is called *eine Autowerkstatt*)
- *das Gift* = poison (a "gift" or "present" is *ein Geschenk*)
- *das Gymnasium* = high school, secondary school (a "gym" is *eine Turnhalle* or *Sporthalle*)
- *konsequent* = consistent ("consequently" is *folglich* or *als Folge*)
- *das Menü* = today's special in a restaurant (a "menu" is *eine Speisekarte*)
- *der Oldtimer* = an antique car (not used for people)
- *Reformhaus* = health food or natural food store
- *See* = sea (*die See*) or lake (*der See*)—the gender of the word makes all the difference!
- *Slip* = briefs; underwear that just slips on and off (a woman's "slip" is *das Unterkleid* or *der Unterrock*)
- *Slipper* = loafer, shoe without laces (a "slipper" is a *Pantoffel* or *Hausschuh*)
- *Warenhaus* = department store; also called *ein Kaufhaus* (a "warehouse" is a *Lagerhaus*)

Related Web link: http://german.about.com
/library (E)

Preserving the Language: Is It German, English, or Gernglish?

That German talking on his *Handy* (cell phone) is using the CityRate while standing in line at the post office to send a Pack-Set. Many Germans take out a BahnCard to purchase a train ticket for the high-speed InterCity Express (ICE). Germans used to watch *Fernsehen*, a word that has largely given way to *TV* (but at least they pronounce it TAY-FOW). A bestselling German television program guide is named *TV Today*, and the country's number two newsweekly is called *Focus*. (Number one *Der Spiegel* has not yet changed its name to "The Mirror.") The German movie magazine with the biggest circulation bears the title *Cinema*.

Although the English invasion of German has been going on for a long time, some Germans are becoming concerned about the recent barrage of "Gernglish."

The worst *Wortpanscher* (word dilutor) offenders are advertisers. A recent German magazine ad for the U.S. television series "Stargate SG-1" contained more English than German, including the slogan for its beer company sponsor: "The International Taste." Three sentences in a Samsung ad for television sets are in German, but the ad ends with an English slogan: "Challenge the Limits." An ad for Europcar (itself an English name) claims in English: "You rent more than a car." Acer, a British computer firm, splashes across a two-page ad in large yellow letters: "Know How! No Risk! (*Das Knowhow* has been a common "German" word for years.) *Natürlich alles*, including *das* Business Notebook or *der* Miditower, will be configured for you in a "just in time" manner! Ads for the Siemens pocket reader claim it is the world's first "Offline-Textreader."

Despite a report stating that German consumers were put off by English advertising slogans, many German and international companies don't seem to think so. They use English phrases and expressions in their messages to consumers in Austria, Germany, and Switzerland.

Some critics of German "language dilution" have become alarmed enough to ask, "*Gibt es eine Krise der deutschen Sprache?*" ("Is there a German language crisis?") But others point out that German, like most languages, has survived similar linguistic invasions. Historically, both Latin and French have had a powerful impact on German. Such defenders of "English enrichment" are not concerned about German's survival and remind people that during the 17th and 18th centuries French had an even greater influence on German than English does today.

Nevertheless, the Verein Deutsche Sprache (VDS, German Language Association) battles on as the defender of the language. However, when they complain about the new English term for restrooms, *WC Center*, driving out the old word *Toilette*, VDS members ignore the fact that *Toilette* is French, not German.

Related Web links: acer.de—*Acer Corporation's German site* (E, G); **vds-ev.**—Verein Deutsche Sprache (German Language Association) is a group that tries to defend German against English (G); compaq.de/produkte—*Compaq Germany site* (G)

German Words of the Year

Each December the Gesellschaft für deutsche Sprache (GfdS), the German Language Society, announces its selection of the top words of the year. In 1999, the "foreign" word *das Millennium* won the Society's top spot. This Latin-based word, made up of *mille* (thousand) and *annum* (year), largely replaced the Germanic *Jahrtausend* (year + thousand) during the hype leading up to *das Jahr* 2000.

Most of the words in this annual contest can't be found in a dictionary. They are either new coinages or event-related words too recent to be included in any standard German *Wörterbuch*. In 2000 the top word was *Schwarzgeldaffäre* (illegal funds affair), reflecting that year's political fundraising scandal of the CDU party and former German chancellor Helmut Kohl. The second-ranked word for 2000, *BSE-Krise* (mad-cow crisis), came from a major news event of that year. For obvious reasons, the number one choice for 2001 was der 11. September (*der elfte September*).

Like the English expression "A-OK" out of the 1960s, some of these German words fade into relative obscurity. That has already happened to 1999's third-ranked term, *Generation @* (spoken GHEN-ah-RAHT-cee-ohn "at"). It reflected what was happening then and the young generation that has grown up surrounded by the new media and computers. The somewhat artificial word was also the title of the best-selling book, *Generation X*.

The next two German words for 2001 were *Antiterrorkrieg* (war against terrorism), *Milzbrandattacke* (anthrax attack), both related to significant events of that year. For 2000, *Kinderschänder* (child molester) and *Inline-Skating* (a word taken directly from English and criticized for that) made the list. Words selected in 1999 included *Euroland* (the 12 euro-currency countries), *Doppelpass* (dual citizenship passports), *feindliche Übernahme* (hostile takeover), and the nickname "*Sofi*" (for *Sonnenfinsternis*, the solar eclipse). Tenth place went to a special word . . .

Rindfleischetikettierungsüberwachungs-aufgabenübertragungsgesetz won a special award (and tenth position) as the longest German word of 1999. The monster word consisted of 63 letters, 20 syllables, and ten individual words—all to express a law having to do with British beef (*Rindfleisch*) and BSE or "mad cow disease." Although it is a word to strike terror in any German student, the GfdS cited it as a good example of how German can form new words by combining existing ones. It also have been the *Unwort des Jahres*, or the "unword" of the year, a German word or expression that has been overused, misused, or abused. That honor went to *Kollateralschaden* (collateral damage, 1999), *national befreite Zone* (national-free zone, 2000), and *Gotteskrieger* (warrior of God, 2001).

Related Web links: gfds.de—Gesellschaft für deutsche Sprache, the official site of the German Language Society (GfdS) which selects the Words of the Year (G, E); **ids.de**—Institut für deutsche Sprache. The IDS is based in Mannheim (G); **unwortdesjahres.org**—to find the German "unwords" of the year, since 1991 (G)

Language Borrowing: A Little German Here, a Lot of English There

Languages are always borrowing words from each other. English has adopted and adapted many words from French, German, and other languages. German immigrants and other sources have enriched English with numerous words of German heritage. Young children attend a kindergarten (children's garden). At Christmas, they eagerly await Kriss Kringle (a corruption of *Christkindl*, the German giver of Christmas gifts). *Gesundheit* doesn't really mean "bless you"; it means "health" —the good variety being implied. Psychiatrists speak of angst (fear) and practice Gestalt (form) psychology. When something is broken, it's kaput. Although not every English speaker knows that *Fahrvergnügen* is "driving pleasure," most do know that *Volkswagen* means "people's car." Musical works can have a leitmotiv. Our cultural view of the world is called a weltanschauung by historians or philosophers. Similar Germanic terms are commonly understood by most well-read English speakers.

Other words that are borrowed from German include blitz, cobalt, dachshund, delicatessen, ersatz, frankfurter, glockenspiel, hinterland, infobahn (for "information highway"), kaffeeklatsch, pilsner, pretzel, quartz, rucksack, sauerkraut, schnapps, strudel, waltz, and wiener. And from Low German we find brake, dote, and tackle.

Such borrowing is usually a two-way street. The German language, particularly since World War II (which also gave us the blitzkrieg), has likewise taken over the use of many English words—and even some pseudo-English words of which English speakers have never heard.

Many English words have become such an integral part of German that their English origins have largely been forgotten. Even the German Language Association has thrown in the towel on "German" words such as *der Award, das Baby, babysitten* (to babysit), *der Babysitter, das Bodybuilding, das Callgirl, der Camp, der Clown, der Cocktail, der Computer, fit* (in good shape), *die Garage, das Hobby, der Job, jobben* (work), *joggen* (to jog), *killen* (to kill), *der Killer, der Lift* (elevator), *managen* (to manage), *der Manager, das Musical, der Playboy, der Pullover, der Rum, der Smog, der Snob, der Streik* (strike), *das Team, der Teenager, das Ticket, der Trainer* (coach), and *der Tunnel*.

It may also be too late to protect German against the invasion of the possessive apostrophe, as in "Maria's Buch."

Pseudo-English Terms

The following are terms that many German speakers believe to be actual English words but that really exist only in German:

die Basecap = baseball cap

der Dressman = male model

der Fuzzy (Fuzzis) = a strange character or type

das Handy = cellular or mobile telephone

das Happy-End = happy ending in a movie

das Lifting = a face-lift or other plastic surgery

der Smoking = tuxedo, formal dinner jacket

der Talkmaster = talk show host

der Twen = someone in his or her 20s, as in *"Teens und Twens"*

German Radio and TV: Public Versus Private

Since a 1986 court opinion, Germany has had a dual broadcasting system, similar to Great Britain's, in which both private and public broadcasters have access to the airways, communications satellites, and cable transmissions. Germany's public broadcasting corporations (ARD and ZDF) are subject to supervision by three regulatory bodies: the Radio/Television Council (Rundfunk/Fernsehrat), the Administrative Council (Verwaltungsrat), and the Director General. The Radio/Television Council members are either elected by the 16-state (*Land*) parliaments or chosen by the political parties. The representatives must come from a variety of political, religious, and social groups. The council, which is to remain free of governmental influences, advises the Director General on programming issues. The Administration Council determines the budget and supervises the management.

As fair as the German system may sound in theory, German broadcasting is subject to the same political influences and biases that exist in any other country. When they were in power, Chancellor Kohl and his CDU party often objected to what they termed "bias in the media"—a phrase that also sounds familiar to Americans. Kohl's government, unhappy with German television coverage, at one time even threatened to change the broadcast laws. Notwithstanding, Germany's public and private broadcasters remain at least as unfettered as those in most other free, democratic countries. Despite some recent censorship moves, particularly regarding the Internet, Germany still ranks high in its degree of media freedom.

To pay for its public broadcasting services, Germany (like Austria and Switzerland) imposes an annual tax on radio and television sets—but it's called a "fee" (*Gebühr*). This so-called GEZ fee can be paid monthly, quarterly, or annually. The public ARD (radio and television) and ZDF (television) networks each receive 50 percent of these GEZ revenues, in addition to limited advertising income.

Should you be considering not registering your television or radio, be aware that locator trucks cruise through German towns looking for televisions that are turned on but not registered. Watching television in this illegal manner is called *Schwarzfernsehen* and is subject to fines if you get caught.

Related Web links: German television channels (G): ard.de—ARD; sdv.fr/arte—Arte; kabel1.de—Kabel 1; mdr.de—Mitteldeutsche Rundfunk; premiereworld.de—Premiere; prosieben.de—Pro Sieben; rtl.de—RTL; rtl2.de—RTL 2; sat1.de—Sat 1; neunlive.de—TM3; vh1.de—VH-1; vh1.de—ZDF online
Popular television shows (G): sat1.de/haraldschmidt—"Die Harald Schmidt Show," the German David Letterman, lindenstrasse.de—"Lindenstraße," ARD cult soap; das-erste.de/marie—"Marienhof," ARD Cologne-based soap; tagesschau.de—"Tagesschau," ARD news
Other sites: eurotv.com—EuroTV, guide to European channels, including Germany (E); kabel-tv.de—Kabel-TV (G); gez.de—GEZ payment site (G)

FSK—Film Ratings and Culture

Film censorship is as old as the film industry. So, while Germany has a long history of film censorship and film ratings, so do most other countries. Unlike the United Kingdom's BBFC, the Motion Picture Association of America claims that its ratings are merely guidelines, not censorship. Regardless, any movie rating system ends up being a kind of censorship, even if it claims otherwise, and the German rating system is no different.

In Germany, movie censorship began in Berlin in 1906 when the chief of police announced that all films would be subject to *Präventivzensur*, meaning they had to be screened and approved in advance of any public showing. In 1920, the German government passed the *Reichslichtspielgesetz*, or Imperial Motion Picture Law, that called for the approval (*Freigabe*) of any film to be exhibited anywhere in the Reich. During the Nazi era, strict control of the film industry and film distribution meant that any motion picture shown in Germany had a government seal of approval. Since 1949, all movies shown in Germany have been rated by the FSK (Freiwillige Selbstkontrolle der Filmwirtschaft). Despite its name, the FSK "Voluntary Self-Regulation of the Film Industry" is not at all voluntary. No film or video made in Hollywood, Germany, or anywhere else can be distributed in Germany without an FSK rating.

A country's film-rating system can reveal a lot about its culture. The first thing you notice in a comparison of Anglo-American versus German film ratings is the different emphasis placed on two important criteria: sex and violence. In contrast to the U.S. system, the FSK approves films with "mild sexual situations" for ages 12 and above (*freigegeben ab 12 Jahren*). But a film with violent scenes usually can't be viewed by anyone under 16.

Germany's film-rating system skirts the German constitution's unambiguous statement that "no censorship shall take place" partly by falling under the country's *Jungendschutzgesetze*, its youth-protection laws.

FSK RATINGS

- *ohne Altersbeschränkung*—all ages admitted
- *ab 6*—age 6 and up
- *ab 12*—age 12 and up
- *ab 16*—age 16 and up
- *ab 18*—age 18 and up
- *Indiziert*—"indexed" films (mostly gory horror and violent porn), which are for adults only and can't be advertised or sold by mail; for DVD and video

Films can be banned entirely. Some 250 films are currently banned in Germany, which means they can't be sold or shown.

Related Web links: fsk.de—official site of the German film-ratings board (G); bbfc.co.uk—British Board of Film Classification (E); mpaa.org—Motion Picture Association of America (E)

The German Press

Even in the age of the Internet, television, and multimedia, Germans continue their love affair with newspapers and magazines. Germany has long been a nation of readers, with one of Europe's highest rates of daily newspaper circulation per capita. In line with a worldwide trend, however, that rate has been declining, from 417 per 1,000 in 1995 to 300 per 1,000 in 2000. That still puts Germany ahead of Australia and the United States, but it falls behind the United Kingdom.

Article 5 of the German *Grundgesetz* (Basic Law, the German constitution) guarantees freedom of the press and the right of access to information. According to watchdog group Freedom House, Germany ranks among the countries of the world that enjoy relatively unfettered freedom of the print and broadcast media. But German journalists do not claim to be "unbiased" or "objective" in their reporting. The newspapers for which they work are generally expected to have a particular political viewpoint ranging from liberal to conservative, or from far left to far right. On the whole, German readers are well aware of each publication's political bent.

The German print media also range from the so-called *Boulevardpresse*, led by the sensational daily *Bild* with its 4.3 million circulation, to the highly respected weekly *Die Zeit*. One of the publishers of *Die Zeit* is Germany's former chancellor (1974–81) Helmut Schmidt.

German (and European) attitudes about nudity mean that you are much more likely to see photos or ads with bare-breasted women in a mainstream German publication such as *Stern* or even *Der Spiegel* than in a comparable U.S. publication.

Major German Newspapers and Magazines (average circulation, 2000)

NEWSPAPERS (ZEITUNGEN)

Berliner Zeitung (daily) 205,000

Bild-Zeitung (Berlin, Hamburg, daily) 4.3 million

Frankfurter Allgemeine (FAZ) (Frankfurt, daily) 400,000

Süddeutsche Zeitung (Munich, daily) 400,000

Westdeutsche Allgemeine Zeitung (Ruhr, daily) 750,000

Die Zeit (Hamburg, weekly) 490,000

MAGAZINES (ZEITSCHRIFTEN)

Das Beste (*Reader's Digest*, monthly) 1.1 million

Bunte (Hamburg, illustrated weekly) 719,000

Focus (Munich, news weekly) 750,000

Der Spiegel (Hamburg, news weekly) 1.1 million

Stern (Hamburg, illustrated weekly) 1.1 million

Related Web links: German newspapers (G): **bild.de**—*Bildzeitung*; **faz.net**—*Frankfurter Allgemeine*, **welt.de**—*Die Welt*, **woche.de**—*Die Woche*

German magazines (G): **dasbeste.de**—*Das Beste/Reader's Digest*; **bunte.de**—*Bunte*; **focus.de**—*Focus*; **spiegel.de**—*Der Spiegel*; **stern.de**—*Stern*; **sueddeutsche.de**—*Süddeutsche Zeitung*

From Bonn to Berlin: Not Even the "Berlin Republic" Can Avoid Germany's Past

The two cities of Bonn and Berlin could hardly be more different: Sleepy Bonn on the banks of the Rhine, bustling Berlin on the banks of the Spree. Bonn—whose name derives from the Celtic *bona* (city)— a onetime Roman outpost. Berlin—from the Slavic word for "fishing settlement"— a place the Romans never saw because it wasn't even there when they were.

On Wednesday, November 25, 1998, the newly elected Chancellor Gerhard Schröder convened the first German cabinet meeting held in Berlin in 50 years. In doing so, the chancellor was making a symbolic gesture expressing his displeasure over the many delays that plagued the official transfer of the German government from Bonn to Berlin. And, as is often the case in Germany, there was no escaping the past. Schröder's cabinet meeting was held in a building formerly occupied by Erich Honecker, the late Communist leader of the now-defunct East German state.

Schröder was impatient to make the move to Berlin and inaugurate the new era of a "Berlin Republic." Back in 1995, after heated debate, the German Bundestag committed itself by a narrow vote to move the German seat of government to Berlin no later than 2003. Soon after that milestone vote, construction began on the new or renovated buildings that the move demanded. In the meantime, to save money, some of Germany's ministries and governmental agencies were forced to move into existing structures—many haunted by ghosts from both the Communist and Nazi eras.

Most non-Germans fail to grasp the deep split that the Bonn-Berlin debate once caused among the country's citizens. After more than five decades, most Germans had grown accustomed to having their capital in the sleepy backwater that was Bonn. The quiet university town also had the advantage of being far away from Berlin and its dark legacy of German nationalism run amok. Moving the capital back to Berlin meant a face-to-face confrontation with the city's—and the country's—past. As opponents of the move predicted, the transfer has been a costly affair, but Berlin has acted like a magnet, inexorably attracting more and more government institutions and agencies to the capital.

With the postwar loss of Berlin as its capital, Germany had become a country without a central major metropolis. France had Paris, England had London, but Berlin was a virtual island surrounded and isolated by Communist East Germany. Most of the city's former roles were taken over by several other German cities: Bonn (capital), Frankfurt (banking), Hamburg (publishing), Munich (movies). After a 50-year identity crisis, Berlin is now reestablishing its role in the new Germany.

Related Web links: berlin-info.de—all about the German capital (E, G); **bundestag.de**— Bundestag/Parliament (G)

Berlin's Straße des 17 Juni cuts through the Tiergarten park to the Brandenburg Gate.

From Reichswehr to *Bundeswehr*: The German Armed Forces

Germany's *Bundeswehr* (federal defense force) consists of the army (*Bundesheer*), air force (*Luftwaffe*), and navy (*Bundesmarine*). Because of the Nazi era and tainted past of the military after World War II, Germany and the Allies wanted to avoid associations with the former Reichswehr and Hitler's Wehrmacht. Consequently, members of the military are considered "citizens in uniform" and are guaranteed constitutional rights.

In 1956, Germany imposed mandatory military service for all males over 18. The required term of service has varied from 15 months to the current 10 months (since 1996). Conscientious objectors (*Kriegsverweigerer*) can meet the draft requirement by doing public service in public institutions, but they must serve three months longer than those in military service.

Until recently, women in the military were limited to service in noncombat areas: medical and music. Germany's Basic Law constitution explicitly prevented women from bearing arms, but in October 2000, the Bundestag revised Article 12a to read that women could not be "compelled" to bear arms, thus allowing women to voluntarily do so. On July 2, 2001, for the first time in German history, 677 women began military service along with men in the armed forces.

After World War II, there were two German armed forces, one in the East and one in the West. The Nationale Volksarmee (NVA) of the German Democratic Republic was disbanded after German reunification in 1990 and merged with the western *Bundeswehr*.

Germany has been a member of NATO (North Atlantic Treaty Organization) since 1955, the same year that East Germany's NVA became part of the Soviet-led Warsaw Pact, and Germany's armed forces still constitute the largest single contingent of NATO troops in Europe. Allied/NATO troops from six nations were stationed in Germany, but in the years following reunification and the end of the Cold War, the U.S., British, French, and other troops have largely been withdrawn. In the 1990s, reunified Germany had to face its new military role as the European Union's largest and most influential country. Already in the 1980s, Germany had begun to debate the Basic Law's limitations on where and how German troops could serve. The Helmut Kohl government, reacting to outside criticism that Germany was not pulling its weight militarily, had slowly increased German participation in NATO operations, including the Persian Gulf War in 1991. It was not until 1994, though, that Germany's highest court ruled that German forces could participate in United Nations and joint UN-NATO peacekeeping missions with Bundestag approval. As a result, German troops were stationed in Kosovo in 1999 and in Afghanistan in 2002.

Related Web links: heer.bundeswehr.de— Bundeswehr, Heer (army) (E, G); luftwaffe.de— Luftwaffe (air force) (G); deutschemarine.de— Bundesmarine (navy) (G); gundeswehr.de—for information on all three services

September 11 and Germany

The German reaction to the terrorist attacks of September 11, 2001, tells a lot about the U.S.–German relationship. Much like a death in the family, the German response has gone through several phases.

Although later estimates put the number of German citizens who perished in the disaster (4 of them on airplanes) at 31, initial news reports stated as many as 100. A number of German firms, including Deutsche Bank, had offices in the World Trade Center, and fortunately most of their employees managed to escape harm. But like much of the world, Germans felt deep sympathy for America and Americans following the attacks. They were deeply shaken by the catastrophic events in New York, Washington, and Pennsylvania. Germans—many of whom still feel a strong connection to the country that vanquished them in war but responded with food and support when the war ended—reacted by filling churches for memorial services, flying flags at half mast, holding vigils, and even canceling soccer games. Americans living in Germany and those elsewhere with German friends were almost taken aback by the outpouring of sympathy and heartfelt condolences from their German friends.

That meant even more than the equally heartfelt condolences from German chancellor Gerhard Schröder and other German officials to the American people. But Schröder did more than talk. After a visit to New York City to view the destruction firsthand, Herr Schröder and the German government sponsored a special program that brought 1,000 New York City high school students who lived near to and witnessed the horror of September 11th to Germany for a tour of Berlin and other attractions. More significantly, the German government also sent troops to Afghanistan for peacekeeping support, a move that did not have universal support from the German public.

Later German and international reaction was less sympathetic. President Bush's "axis of evil" comments in his State of the Union address in January 2002 were not well received by most Germans, or by most Europeans. Chancellor Schröder, a strong supporter of the U.S. *Antiterrorfeldzug* (antiterrorism campaign), found himself having to defend Bush's remarks. The German media portrayed Bush and the United States as a western sheriff ignoring the Europeans and acting unilaterally. German Foreign Minister Joschka Fischer declared that Germany and the other allies in the war against terrorism were not "lackeys" of the United States. But in February 2002, the German Media Prize was presented to former New York Mayor Rudolph Giuliani in ceremonies in Baden-Baden, with students from New York in attendance.

Related Web links: bundesregierung.de—the official German government site has up-to-date information on German foreign policy and other matters (G, E); bka.de—the BKA site has information on Germany's own antiterrorism investigations (G)

Political Parties: "Traffic-Light" Coalitions

In the 1998 election, German politics underwent a dramatic change. When the 16-year-long Kohl era ended on election day, Sunday, September 27, and Germany's Sozialistische Partei Deutschlands (SPD, the Social Democrats) returned to power under Gerhard Schröder, it signaled a turning point almost as profound as the collapse of the Berlin Wall and the start of German reunification on November 9, 1989.

The "Union"—the joint name for Kohl's conservative Christliche Demokratische Union (CDU) and the southern German Christliche Sozialistische Union (CSU)—had held the SPD at bay and out of power for so long that most Germans, especially younger ones, had begun to forget the heyday of the SPD in the1970s, when names such as Willy Brandt and Helmut Schmidt were well known. Although most European countries were ruled (and are still ruled) by center-left governments, Germany was ruled by the center-right CDU/CSU and the conservative chancellor Helmut Kohl. In fact, the victory of Chancellor Gerhard Schröder and the socialists has been compared to the similar triumph of Prime Minister Tony Blair and the Labor party over the Tories in Britain.

The 1998 election also gave Germany its "word of the year": *Rot-Grün* (Red-Green). This colorful term for the coalition government made up of the Social Democrats (red) and the Alliance 90/The Greens (green) was proclaimed the number one word of 1998 by the German Language Society and a jury made up of writers, literary critics, and media people.

"Traffic-light coalition" was another popular political phrase. It referred to the red-yellow-green coalitions in some areas of Germany, the yellow symbolizing the Frei Demokratische Partei (FDP), which has had trouble maintaining its minimum 5 percent threshold in recent years.

Related Web links: German parties (G): **spd.de**— Sozialistische Partei Deutschlands; **cdu.de**— Christliche Demokratische Union; **csu.de**— Christliche Sozialistische Union; **gruene.de**— Bündnis 90/Die Grüne; **liberale.de**—Frei Demokratische Partei (FDP)

General: **politik-digital.de**—German politics online (G)

The renovated Reichstag, with its new glass dome, draws tourists from all over the world.

The Religious Split: From Pagan Unity to Christian Division

Around A.D. 350, the Visigoth bishop Ulfilas (Wulfila) completed the first translation of the Bible into *Gotisch*, an early form of German. By the second half of the eighth century, all of the pagan Germanic peoples had been Christianized. Today Germany's population is almost evenly split between Roman Catholics (*römischkatholisch*) and Protestants (*evangelisch*). Although most of the Catholics live in Bavaria in southern Germany, and the Protestants in north Germany, there are pockets of Catholicism in the Rhineland northern cities such as Cologne (Köln), while the southwestern state of Baden-Württemberg is largely Protestant. Muslims, Jews, and people of other minority faiths make up less than 4 percent of Germany's population.

Germany was home to the Protestant Reformation, which began in Wittenberg in 1517 when Martin Luther expressed his objections to the church practice of selling indulgences, by tacking his "95 Theses" to the door of Wittenberg's All Saints church (as legend has it). The Reformation continued in Germany as well as Switzerland by Philipp Melanchthon (Augsburg), Huldrych Zwingli (Zurich), John Calvin (Geneva), and other reformers. By 1526, the Protestants were already split into the Reformed and Lutheran divisions. In 1530, Melanchthon drafted the Augsburg Confession (Augsburger Bekenntnis), the "constitution" of both the Lutheran faith and the Schmalkaldic League.

It is an irony of history that in eastern Germany, the location of *die Lutherstadt Wittenberg*, the city most identified with the Reformer, traditional religion virtually died out during the Communist years. The East German government was amazingly successful in stamping out the "opiate of the people" and replacing it with many secular practices including the secular *Jugendweihe* confirmation.

Religion is a compulsory subject in German secondary schools. Separate classes are taught for Protestants and Catholics (and in some cases for Jews and Muslims). For others there is an ethics course (*Ethik*). Students over the age of 14 can opt out of religious or ethical instruction.

Although today the influence of the Mormons, born-again Christians, and other "sects" as well as growing numbers of Islamic faithful can be seen, most German speakers, even those who consider themselves Protestant or Catholic, rarely set foot in a house of worship.

Protestant

The word *Protestant* comes from the second imperial Diet of Speyer in 1529. A minority opinion, a *protestation*, was issued on behalf of those princes who objected to the diet's reversal of a decision by the first Diet of Speyer in 1526 that rulers in the empire could each determine the religion of their own realms. In German, the word *evangelisch* is most often used for "Protestant"—less often *protestantisch*.

Related Web links: ekd.de—Vereinigte Evangelisch-Lutheranische Kirche Deutschlands (United Lutheran Church of God) (G); **dbk.de**—Deutsche Bischofskonferenz, see *Katholische Kirche* (G)

State and Church: *Die Balancierte Trennung*: The Delicate Balance

While Germany has no official state church, as with the Lutheran Church in Sweden, the German government collects "church tax" (*die Kirchensteuer*) from the country's Protestants, Catholics, and Jews (but not from Muslims). Through a unique state-church partnership, the government imposes a tax, via the income tax, to support church schools, churches, and other installations. Although the *Grundgesetz* (German constitution) guarantees religious freedom, this kind of close cooperation between government and church would be considered unconstitutional in the United States and many other countries. But the German brand of state-church cooperation goes beyond the *Kirchensteuer*. German clergy and priests are educated mostly in tax-supported public colleges and universities, and churches have the right to choose the faculty members of departments of theology. For their part, the churches help staff and run schools, hospitals, homes for elderly people (*Altenheime*).

It's logical that in the homeland of Martin Luther, most of Germany's Protestants are Lutheran. Die Evangelische Kirche in Deutschland (EKD, the Protestant Church in Germany), headquartered in Hannover, is an association of 24 largely independent Lutheran churches, the largest being the Augsburg Confession (Augsburger Bekenntnis). The EKD and its members regard non-Lutheran Protestants, *die Freikirchen* (free churches) — Methodists, Mormons, Jehovah's Witnesses, and so forth — as *Sekten* (sects) and not "true" Protestant churches.

The East German Protestant church played a major role in bringing down the Communist German Democratic Republic. Protestant churches all across the GDR became centers for protests that eventually led to the 1989 collapse of East Germany and the fall of the Berlin Wall. Ironically, many eastern Germans have turned their backs on the church that helped win their freedom. The rate of church membership and attendance in the east is considerably lower than in the west.

Following German reunification, the Roman Catholic Church, *die katholische Kirche*, added only 4 East German dioceses (*Bistümer*) or archdioceses (*Erzbistümer*), for a total of 27, after its reorganization in 1994.

Germany's two major faiths get along well, without the serious tensions found in some other parts of the world, actively cooperating at the local, regional, and national levels as well as in international ecumenical organizations such as the World Council of Churches.

The *Kirchensteuer* is collected by the government for the Protestant, Roman Catholic, and Jewish denominations. The church tax amounts to approximately 8 to 9 percent of the income tax for the tax year. Some Germans avoid the church tax by officially leaving the church (not possible in all *Länder*). Foreign nationals are also exempt if they have no official registered religious affiliation. Because German taxpayers can deduct the *Kirchensteuer* from their taxable income, resulting in lost tax revenue, this church support amounts to a government subsidy.

The Bible in German: From Ulfilas to Luther

Essentially, every Bible is a translation (*eine Übersetzung*). The ancient elements that became what we now call the Bible (*die Bibel*) were originally written in Hebrew, Aramaic, and Greek on papyrus, leather, and clay. The earliest Germanic version of the Bible was Ulfilas's Gothic translation from Latin and Greek. From Ulfilas came much of the Germanic Christian vocabulary that is still in use today. Later, in the ninth century, Charlemagne (Karl der Große) fostered Frankish (Germanic) translations. Over the years, prior to the appearance of the first printed German Bible in 1466, various German and German dialect translations of the Scriptures were published. The *Augsburger Bibel* of 1350 was a complete New Testament; the Wenzel Bible (1389) contained the Old Testament in German.

Johannes Gutenberg's famous 42-line Bible, printed in Mainz, was in Latin. About 40 copies exist today in various states of completeness. It was Gutenberg's invention of printing from movable type that made the Bible, in any language, vastly more influential and important by making possible the production of books in greater quantities at a lower cost.

In 1466, before Martin Luther was even born, a German Bible that was a literal translation of the Latin Vulgate was published using Gutenberg's invention of movable type. Known as the Mentel Bible, it was printed in Strasbourg and appeared in some 18 editions until it was replaced by Luther's new translation in 1522.

The most influential German Bible, and the one that continues to be most widely used in the Germanic world (last official revised edition in 1984), was translated from the original Hebrew and Greek by Martin Luther (1483–1546) in the record time of just 10 weeks (New Testament), during his involuntary stay in the Wartburg Castle in Wittenberg. Luther's first complete Bible in German appeared in 1534. He continued to revise his translations up until his death. In response to Luther's Protestant Bible, the German Catholic Church published its own versions, most notably the *Emser Bibel*, which became the standard German Catholic Bible. Luther's German Bible also became the primary source for other northern European versions in Danish, Dutch, and Swedish.

In 1524, having been barred by church authorities from creating a new English version of the Bible in England, the English scholar and translator William Tyndale went to Germany. Financed by London merchants, Tyndale's translation of the New Testament was published in Cologne in 1525, and later in Worms. Copies of his new translation reached England in 1526, but Tyndale paid a high price for his efforts. Before he could complete his work on the Old Testament, he was captured in Belgium and later burned at the stake (1536) for his "untrue translations." His Bibles were burned, but his work proved to be a lasting influence on English Bible translation in later centuries, including the venerable King James Version of 1611.

German Jews

In the years just prior to World War II, Germany was home to about 530,000 Jews. Today, out of a total population of 81 million, only about 61,000 Germans are members of Jewish congregations in Germany, along with 10,000 estimated nonmembers. Since the registered Jewish population was only about 28,000 in 1990, most of those in Germany today are recent Eastern European and Russian Jewish arrivals. With the country's having such a low Jewish population, few Germans have ever known a Jew personally. Despite this fact, the issue of Jews and their history in Germany continues to dominate many aspects of the German religious, cultural, and political landscape. Jews and Jewish issues are featured much more prominently in the German media than the population numbers would indicate, especially when compared with Germany's largest religious minority, the 3.2 million Muslims (mostly Turks).

Germany's Jewish community is represented by the Central Council of Jews in Germany (Zentralrat der Juden in Deutschland), which has its headquarters in Bonn. The German Institute for Jewish Studies (die Hochschule für Jüdische Studien) was established in 1980 in Heidelberg. The *Zentralarchiv*, a large archive for research on the history of the Jews in Germany, was established in 1987, also in Heidelberg. Ignatz Bubis, the head of the *Zentralrat* from 1992 until his death in 1999, was often seen on television and in the news commenting on various issues.

It is in Berlin that today's Jewish presence is most apparent. Almost one in five of the country's Jews lives in the German capital. The new, starkly appealing Jewish Museum by the Polish-American architect Daniel Libeskind became a popular destination even before its exhibits were completed. The landmark Jewish synagogue (Neue Synagoge, built in 1866) on Oranienburger Straße has been beautifully restored. Work on Berlin's controversial holocaust memorial began in October 2001 on a four-acre site not far from the Reichstag.

Berlin in the 1920s had a thriving community of liberal Reform Jews who were trying to change from the traditional Orthodox ways (more participation by women, organs in synagogues, and so forth). That all ended with the Nazis and the war, and today most of Germany's Jews (few of them born in Germany) are either Orthodox or nonpracticing. On the bright side, Berlin has again become the center of progressive or Reform Judaism in Germany. However, the Jewish factions are facing the issue of tax support, since only Orthodox Judaism is considered Germany's official Jewish group and thus receives all church-tax funding.

> **Related Web links:** hagalil.com/brd/berlin/jewish.htm—Jews in Berlin (E, G); hagalil.com/juedisches-museum—Jewish Museum in Berlin (E, G); berlin-judentum.de—Jewish Berlin (E, G)

Germany and Scientology: Persecution or Objectivity?

The word *sect* (*die Sekte*) in German carries much the same negative tone as *cult* in English (also *der Kult* in German) but with added implications of illegality and fraud. *Eine Sekte* is just about any Christian religious group that is not a part of the two mainstream German churches, the Catholics and the Lutherans. Although the word applies to Baptists, Methodists, Mormons, Presbyterians, and other "sects" in Germany and other German-speaking countries, it is more often used to refer to Jehovah's Witnesses (*die Zeugen Jehovas*) and, particularly, the Church of Scientology in Germany.

While Germans tend to look askance at any "sect," the Church of Scientology has been targeted for attacks by German church leaders, lawmakers, and private citizens. Ever since the American founder of Scientology, L. Ronald Hubbard, opened the first offices in Hamburg back in 1970, Scientology has been a lightning rod.

Books accusing the Church of Scientology of everything from being a danger to the German economy to "psychological terrorism" and the use of kidnapping and extortion have often been on German bestseller lists. There are several German anti-Scientology websites, at least one of them an "official" site run by the state of Nordrhein-Westfalen. State and federal government agencies have implemented bans against Scientologists. In 1996, the state of Bavaria barred anyone connected with Scientology from holding government jobs. Berlin requires contractors for state work to declare that they have no ties to Scientology. Even the U.S. delivery service UPS has been accused by a German consumer group of financially supporting the Church of Scientology. One might think that there are millions of Scientologists in Germany, while in fact estimates range from a mere 30,000 to 70,000.

Not that Scientology is without its critics in other places, but the degree of persecution and prosecution in Germany has led to accusations of Nazi-like religious intolerance, especially after anti-Scientology boycotts in 1996 against the film *Mission Impossible* and actor Tom Cruise. (The movie was still a big hit in Germany.) Such moves led to an unsuccessful series of newspaper ads in the *International Herald Tribune* and the *New York Times* (no German papers would carry the ads) that attempted to cast Germany's persecution of Scientology in the same light as German anti-Jewish attacks of the 1930s. In a country where it is illegal to display the Nazi swastika or to sell a copy of *Mein Kampf*, such comparisons only served to increase the level of anti-Scientology sentiment.

Related Web links: cisar.org—German Scientology News, an anti-Scientology site (E); snafu.de/~tilman—The Cult of Greed and Power: $cientology, another German anti-Scientology site (E, G); verfassungsschutz.nrw.de—Verfassungsschutz-NRW, a government "constitutional protection" site that has an anti-Scientology section (G); scientology.org—Church of Scientology (E)

Aspirin® or aspirin? A Classic Medicine and a Lost Trademark

Aspirin (*das Aspirin*) marked its 100th birthday in 1997. Although some two thousand years ago, the Greek Hippocrates knew of the painkilling properties of aspirin's main natural ingredient, which is extracted from the bark of willow trees, it was a German chemist who invented what we now know as aspirin, on August 10, 1897. Dr. Felix Hoffmann, in the employ of Bayer AG's predecessor Farbenfabriken vormals Friedr. Bayer & Co, was attempting to find an improved pain reliever for his father's arthritis when he discovered acetylsalicylic acid (ASA; *Azetylsalizylsäure*, or ASS, in German). The new compound was named "aspirin" as a result of combining the *a* in *Azetyl-*, *spir* from the Latin/Greek-based *Spirsäure* (salicylic acid, for the plant genus *Spiraea*, in which this natural acid is found), and the Latin *in*, for "found in." But Bayer (BYE-er) didn't register its new drug with the Imperial Patent Office in Berlin, or market it, until 1899.

Neither Hippocrates nor Hoffmann knew how aspirin's key ingredient performs its magic. Another 74 years went by before ASA's secrets were revealed by British researcher John Vane in 1971. (For his discovery, Vane received the 1982 Nobel Prize in medicine.) And more than a century after Felix Hoffmann's synthesis of acetylsalicylic acid, this longtime staple of medicine cabinets around the globe continues to amaze. The more that modern science reveals about aspirin, the more miraculous it seems. Since the 1960s, it has been used in the treatment of thrombosis and other blood-clotting ailments. More recently, aspirin has gained new respect for its preventive effects against strokes, heart attacks, and possibly even some cancers.

This does not mean that the wonder analgesic is for everyone. Some people are allergic to aspirin, and it has been linked to gastrointestinal irritation and the more serious Reye's syndrome. Yet, despite more recent competitors such as acetaminophen and ibuprofen, aspirin can still claim benefits that other drugs can't, particularly for certain heart conditions.

Although Bayer's old invention is still a valid registered trademark in at least 70 countries, in the United States and many other nations, *aspirin* long ago became a generic term, and Bayer lost its legal claim to the word that the company had coined.

These days, Bayer's aspirin plant in Bitterfeld churns out about a third of the world's total 50,000 tons of aspirin each year. Nevertheless, you can't buy a bottle of aspirin over the counter in Germany. As explained in the "Health and Fitness" chapter, in the land of its invention (and in Austria and Switzerland), aspirin is available only in an *Apotheke* (pharmacy, chemist's shop). And you'll need to ask for it by its trademarked name, Aspirin.

Related Web links: bayer.de—Bayer AG (E, G); bayeraspirin.com—Bayer, Inc. (E)

Germans in Space: *Deutsche im Weltall*

You may know that a German astronaut (*Raumfahrer*) was on board the February 2000 NASA space shuttle mission to map the earth in 3-D. But do you know who the first German in space was? Well, neither do most Germans. It happened in 1978, and the answer is in the following discussion.

Neither the Russian nor the American space programs would have got off the ground as quickly as they did without the talents and experience of the rocket scientists they imported from occupied Germany at the end of World War II. (Wernher von Braun on the U.S. side is probably the most famous.) So, it seems only fair that both the Russians and the Americans have invited Germans (and the Swiss Claude Nicolier) to participate in their space missions over the years. In February 2000, Dr. Gerhard P. J. Thiele was on board the *Raumfähre Endeavour* for NASA's STS-99 Shuttle Radar Topography Mapping Mission (SRTM). Thiele, who was born in Germany on September 2, 1953, is a trained physicist. He began working for the DLR (Deutsches Zentrum für Luft- und Raumfahrt, the German Aerospace Center) and undergoing astronaut training in 1988. He joined the European Space Authority in 1998 after having completed NASA's Astronaut Candidate Training program at the Johnson Space Center, in Texas.

In addition to a German astronaut, the technology on board the SRTM mission was German. The 3-D mapping flight was a cooperative project of NASA, NIMA (National Imagery and Mapping Agency),

the DLR, and the ASI (Italian Space Agency). The German company Dornier Satellitensysteme GmbH, part of Daimler-Chrysler Aerospace (Dasa), in Munich, was the main contractor for the X-SAR radar system used on the mission.

Before Gerhard Thiele, nine other Germans had already gone into space—on either American or Russian spacecraft. All but two of the German astronauts have been physicists. In 1978, the East German army officer Sigmund Jähn became the first German in orbit, on board the Soviet spacecraft *Soyuz 31*. Along with the Soviet commander, Jähn linked up with and went aboard the space station (*Raumstation*) *Salyut 6*. In 1983, the first West German astronaut, Ulf Merbold, made two trips aboard the U.S. space shuttle *Columbia*.

The German-American Wernher von Braun (1912–77) served as the first director of NASA's Marshall Space Flight Center from 1960 to 1970. Von Braun became a U.S. citizen in 1955, just two years before the Jupiter C rocket he had developed carried the first U.S. satellite (Explorer 1) into earth orbit. The historic 1969 Apollo 11 moon landing was largely made possible by the German V-2 rocket background of Wernher von Braun and the giant Saturn V rocket that he and his team at NASA developed.

Related Web links: dlr.de—German Aerospace Center (E, G); **jsc.nasa.gov/bios/htmlbios/ thiele.html**—NASA's biographical data on Gerhard Thiele (G)

Das Handy Might Not Be So Handy

The "German" word for a mobile or cellular phone, *das Handy*, is unfamiliar to the majority of English speakers, but one of every two Germans uses a *Handy*. Digital wireless service was introduced earlier and more widely in Europe than in North America. European cell phone carriers also offer features that are either not widely available in North America or were introduced there later, including speech recognition and wireless Internet access. Another European feature enjoyed by few Americans: the caller pays for calls to cell phones. But Europe's wireless lead has been fading as new technologies bring the wireless phone and the handheld computer closer together.

Unfortunately, even the newest of the world's mobile phone systems aren't always compatible. A German who takes a *Handy* along on a business trip to the United States may discover that it is quite useless in the New World. The same is true for an American taking a cell phone to Germany or any other country on that side of the Atlantic. The problem is that several different basic wireless phone-system technologies are in use throughout the world, and only a few are used in both Germany and non-European locations. Attempts to achieve a worldwide mobile phone standard have been thwarted by various competing technology companies and political interests. Other than more expensive satellite phones, there is no global wireless phone standard that will work anywhere on the planet.

On the positive side, the GSM (Global System for Mobile) communications standard used throughout Europe means that a German *Handy* will work as well in Italy or Austria as it does in Germany. Another plus for the GSM system is that most GSM phones also take advantage of SIM card technology, incorporating a smart card that can be inserted in the phone to allow the use of more than one phone number. This enables a U.S. or Canadian businessperson in Germany to receive calls using a North American phone number, as well as the phone's European number.

Although GSM is a single standard, its various iterations use different wave bands. Germany has two main systems, known as the D-Netz (D1 and D2) and the E-Netz. The D-Netz is in the 900-megahertz (MHz) band, while the E-Netz operates at 1,800 MHz. In North America, there are GSM networks operating at 800 and 1,900 MHz. Some phone makers and wireless carriers (Cingular, Voice Stream, AT&T) now offer dual-band or multiband "world phones" that will work in different networks, and even on both sides of the Atlantic. But a cheaper alternative is to simply buy a prepaid *Handy* in Germany.

Related Web links: **dtag.de**—Deutsche Telekom, the main German telecom (E, G); **d2privat.de**— D2 privat, one of the top digital providers (E, G); **eplus.de**—e-plus, one of the top digital providers (E, G); **german-way.com/german/handy.html**— cell phone tips for Germany and Europe (E); **cingular.com**—A U.S. GSM carrier offering world phones (E); **voicestream.com/worldclass**—U.S. carrier that offers GSM world phones (E)

Telefonieren: A Rapidly Changing Telecom Landscape

January 1, 1999, marked a sea change in the German telecommunications market. Its name was deregulation. Ever since, Germans who once were used to dealing with a single, government-run telephone giant have been adjusting to life in a bewildering world of telecom choices. Now that Deutsche Telekom (DT), the country's privatized former phone monopoly, faces real competition, German telephone customers face choices among a virtual galaxy of companies.

The positive result of this new telecom array is that rates in Germany have fallen steadily and dramatically. Even once-stodgy Deutsche Telekom cut its long-distance rates for calls within Germany, and several low-cost competitors now offer even lower rates. The cost of calls outside of Germany varies widely, but most carriers offer lower rates than DT. However, it is difficult to compare rates, since one carrier may have higher rates for certain calling destinations, and lower ones for others.

It is precisely such confusion that has led to another German telecom phenomenon, the so-called telephone broker (*Telefonmakler*). A telephone broker offers to choose the best telecom solution for private or business customers. The service is supported by fees paid by the telecoms to the broker, at no extra cost to the phone customer.

German phone subscribers still pay per-minute charges, even for local calls, since the concept of a flat rate remains something of a novelty. Even though the cost of a local call has dropped considerably, most Germans have not overcome their tradi-tional reluctance to spend large amounts of time on the phone. But as the telecom landscape continues its rapid transformation, some old habits are dying out. Today, despite local phone charges, Germany leads Europe in the number of homes and businesses connected to the Internet. The German online access rate is expected to more than double—from 48 percent (2001)—in the next few years.

> Deutsche Telekom's proclivity for English terms has drawn the ire of Germany's Verein deutsche Sprache. The association objected to DT's practice of labeling its various phone services in English instead of German, such as "freecall," "CityRate," and "GermanCall." Then too, some of DT's so-called English would cause a bit of head shaking in the English-speaking world. Germans now receive phone bills for "sunshine" or "moonshine" rates. According to the Association for the Protection of the German Language, most Germans are unable to understand such terms.

Related Web links: dtag.de—Deutsche Telekom, Germany's traditional phone monopoly is now a public corporation facing increasing telecom competition on many fronts (E, G); **germanway.com/german/teletips.html**—telephone tips, including telephone cards, cell phones, and Internet access (E)

Germany's phone system has undergone great changes in the past
few years.

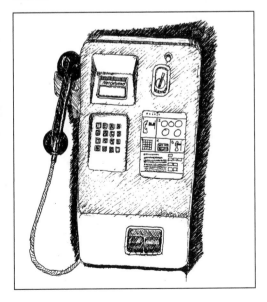

Germans and the Internet: *Wir Surfen das Web!*

Although the United States and the English language continue to dominate the Internet and the World Wide Web, Europe and Japan are also strong contenders. Non-English websites with URLs (uniform resource locators) ending in .jp, .uk, .it, or .de (Germany) are increasing in number every day. According to statistics from StatMarket.com, Global Reach, and other sources, Germany leads Europe in Internet use, with almost twice as many Germans online as in the United Kingdom, the nearest runner-up. Germany ranks fourth behind the United States and Japan among the top 10 countries on the Web, accounting for 6.7 percent of all Internet traffic in 2001. This high rate of usage is all the more impressive given that Germans, like other Europeans, have to pay per-minute phone charges for Internet access. As noted, flat-rate pricing, so common in the United States, is still a relatively new concept in Europe.

However, increasing competition in telecommunications has wrought changes. In October 1999, AOL Europe raised (or lowered) the ladder a little when it began offering a monthly flat rate for unlimited Internet access in Germany. Even so, AOL's German subscribers must also pay 0.02 euro per minute for their "unlimited" time on the Web. Other German telecoms have also offered "Internet by call," in which a Web surfer pays only for the reduced phone charges while online, with no monthly fee.

AOL's German flat rate was in response to competition from Britain's Freeserve and other "free" European Internet service providers (ISPs) that offer Internet access for no fee and at a much lower telephone rate than former state monopolies such as the recently privatized Deutsche Telekom or British Telecom. The number of local and regional German ISPs has also mushroomed in the last several years. (The same is true in Austria and Switzerland.)

The one area where Europeans do not seem to be catching up to Americans on the Web is online shopping. So far, Europeans have been less willing to do their purchasing electronically. This is true even of Germans, despite how limited their shopping hours are in comparison with most of the rest of Europe. Whether out of traditional privacy concerns, reluctance to use credit cards, or reasons unknown, Germans and other Europeans are not big online shoppers, but the German rate of online buying has been on an upward trend.

Top Web Users by Language Other Than English (43.0%)

Japanese	9.2%
Chinese	9.2%
German	**6.7%**
Spanish	6.7%
Korean	4.4%
Italian	3.8%
French	3.3%

Source: Global Reach, September 2001

Related Web link: global-reach.biz/globalstats/index.php3—Global Reach, see *Languages on the Internet* (E)

Society and Social Strata: *Die Oberen Zehntausend*

Is there a German elite? Germans tend to be antielitist. They like to think of their social structure as lacking the large class distinctions that are more obvious in Britain, France, and many other Western countries, but things aren't always what they appear to be.

In recent years, in an effort to cope with increasing diversity in German society, sociologists have struggled to find more valid paradigms than the traditional hierarchy of upper, middle, and lower classes. A further complication for German sociologists is that, up until November 1989, there were two very different German societies that were literally walled off from each other for decades.

With the rise of the service sector in the 1970s and '80s in the West, and as income levels have climbed for most laborers and blue-collar workers, approaching the rate of white-collar earnings, sociologists claim that it is now more important to look at educational backgrounds and what people do with their income, rather than just how much they earn.

Given the country's much-vaunted "social market economy" and a strong system of social welfare, a German's income is less of a factor than it was in earlier times. Nowadays, you may be able to tell more about a German's social status by looking at the car the person drives, where he or she vacations, the newspaper the person reads, how the individual's living room is decorated, or where and what the subject eats and drinks. *Lebensstil* (lifestyle) and *die feinen Unterschiede* (subtle differences) are now key elements of what is *typisch deutsch* — if there is indeed anything that is "typically German" these days. That said, here are some key factors that characterize German society in some way:

• Aside from a few "Ruhr barons" of the past and a media baron or two, there are almost no German Rockefellers or Vanderbilts. The self-made industrial billionaire is a German rarity, and wealthy Germans tend to keep a low profile.

• Germany's small upper elite—the so-called *obere Zehntausend* (upper 10,000)—actually numbers from one thousand to several thousand, or less than 1 percent of the population, according to estimates. Members of this rare breed fall into several categories, including politicians, businesspeople, and union leaders.

• Germany's large *Mittelschicht* (middle class) makes up about two-thirds of the total population, but it is a very diversified group, reflecting many different lifestyles and professions.

• Inequities in job and advancement opportunities continue to exist for minorities and women. Almost no women occupy the upper levels of German business and finance.

Related Web link: bundesregierung.de—this main site of the German government offers information about German society (E, G)

German Citizenship: *Jus Soli Versus Jus Sanguinis*

The world is generally divided into those countries that determine citizenship based on where a person is born (*jus soli*, Latin for "law of the soil"; *Bodenrecht* in German) and those that determine citizenship based on parentage (*jus sanguinis*, Latin for "law of blood"; *Blutsrecht* in German). Germany is among those nations that have citizenship laws based on the latter.

Except for minor amendments, Germany's existing *jus sanguinis* citizenship laws date back to 1914 and a time when the population was much more homogeneous and relatively free of *Ausländer* (foreigners). The *Blutsrecht* principle itself actually goes back to Bavaria in 1818 and went into effect in the German Reich in 1870.

Today's much more *"multi-kulti"* Germany finds itself clashing with the contradictions and inequities that *Blutsrecht* causes in a country that is now home to more than 7 million *Ausländer*, nearly 9 percent of Germany's total population of 82 million. Few of these 7 million permanent residents have German citizenship. The fact that almost one in four of these "foreigners" was born in Germany and acts and talks like any other German has not yet helped them become German citizens. Germany's 2 million Turks, the largest foreign contingent, have long felt discriminated against by the naturalization hurdle.

While a foreigner living in France or Great Britain can apply for citizenship after only 5 years of residence, Germany used to make its foreign nationals wait 15 long years (8 years for children age 16 to 23). Of the 15 EU countries, Germany stood with Austria, Luxembourg, Spain, and Sweden as the only countries that did not grant automatic citizenship to children born in the country. The other 10 not only do so but also allow dual citizenship.

Critics of the strict naturalization laws viewed them as a relic of the past that was preventing the integration and full participation of Germany's foreign citizens. Change came when Gerhard Schröder became chancellor in late 1998. Schröder and his SPD/Green coalition government pushed through more liberal naturalization laws, including dual citizenship, despite the opposition of the CDU/CSU party.

Highlights of Germany's New Citizenship Law

- The time required before a foreigner can apply for citizenship, formerly 15 years, is now 8 years.
- A foreign spouse of a German citizen can apply for citizenship after only 3 years.
- Any child born in Germany automatically becomes a German citizen as long as at least one parent was also born in Germany.
- Foreigners may obtain German citizenship and retain their former citizenship.
- Naturalized citizens must demonstrate that they can speak German and pledge to uphold the German constitution and the democratic system.
- New citizens must prove they have no criminal record, can financially support themselves, and are not likely to end up on welfare assistance.

Muslims and Other Minorities in Germany

When the Turkish grand vizier, Kara Mustapha, tried to take Vienna in 1683, among the forces that defeated the Ottoman Turks were troops from Bavaria, Franconia, Saxony, and Swabia—all now states or regions of Germany. That famous battle on the Kahlenberg Hills had two major results: the end of Turkish invasions of Europe and the start of Austrian and German coffeehouses.

So, there is some irony in the fact that Muslim Turks today are the largest ethnic minority living in Germany. The horrendous terrorist attack on America on September 11, 2001, put a new spotlight on the Muslim population in Germany. As the ensuing investigation focused on Hamburg and possible connections with the al-Quds mosque there, Germany's 2.1 million Muslims, not all of whom are Turks, found themselves under a microscope.

Most people of the Islamic faith in Germany came from Turkey during the wave of guest-worker (*Gastarbeiter*) immigration in the 1960s and '70s, but many of the younger generation were born in Germany and don't even speak Turkish. Kurdish and Arabic (Moroccan, Lebanese, Iraqi, Syrian, and so forth) Muslims are also in Germany. Political tension between the Kurds and the Turks has led to violent demonstrations within Germany. Most Muslims, the third largest religious group in Germany after Catholic and Protestant Christians, live peaceful, ordinary lives. Yet, even before September 11, Turks and other Muslims living in Germany complained of discrimination and being treated as second-class citizens. Until recently, Ger-

man law made it difficult for resident foreigners to become German citizens, even if they had been born there or had lived in the country for many years. Still, many Turkish Germans, such as the writer Akif Pirinçci (*Tränen sind immer das Ende, Felidae*), have been able to be quite successful in German society.

Non-German foreigners living in Germany make up about 9 percent of the population. More than half of them have been living in the country for at least 10 years and almost a third for 20 years or more. Until its liberal asylum laws were toughened in 1993, Germany took in about 80 percent of all asylum seekers in the entire European Union. Minorities within Germany's 7.3 million *Ausländer* population also include Italians, Greeks, Yugoslavs, Serbs, Croats, Sorbs, Roma (Gypsies), and even Americans and British, the latter two nationalities numbering just in excess of 100,000 each.

Related Web links: isoplan.de/aid/2001-2/schwerpunkt.htm—Ausländer in Deutschland: Araber (Foreigners in Germany: Arabs) (G); ruhr-uni-bochum.de/tabo/zdftuerkenin deutschland.htm—Türken in Deutschland (Turks in Germany) (G)

SOCIAL ISSUES AND ATTITUDES
Behinderte: Germans with Disabilities

Any truly organized movement aimed at fighting discrimination against and obtaining improved rights for people with disabilities has been slow to evolve in Germany. In the 1960s, such activities were mostly limited to the field of sports. In the 1970s, according to Germany's Association for Independent Living (ISL), the movement began to take on an increasingly political character and to deal with larger, more general issues concerning people with disabilities. The first tentative steps toward setting up an organization for those purposes were taken at the so-called *Krüppeltribunal* (cripples' tribunal) in 1981 in Düsseldorf. After that first meeting of disabled persons from all over Germany, another five years went by before the actual establishment of the first Zentrum für Selbstbestimmtes Leben (Center for Independent Living) in Bremen.

Critics of Germany's slow progress in the area of improved conditions for people with disabilities point to laws in Sweden, the United States, Canada, and other countries that have greatly enhanced accessibility to buildings, public transportation, and cultural events, and they ask why Germany has been reluctant to pass similar laws. Although there are many international and European recommendations for easier access, these critics say, Germany and some other European countries have failed to take the needed steps to make them a reality.

While some advancement has taken place in the last decade, many German apartment buildings, even those with four or five floors, have no elevator. Only recently did the German railway Deutsche Bahn move to provide wheelchair access in its trains.

Germany's organizations representing disabled persons are trying to persuade German legislators to pass laws that would not only require easy access to buildings but also encourage better social integration and equality for people with special needs and make it possible for them to live more independent lives.

Related Web links: selbsthilfe-online.de— Selbsthilfe der Behinderten, a German organization for the rights of people with disabilities (E, G); cebeef.com—online magazine for people with disabilities (G); isl-ev.org— Interessenvertretung Selbstbestimmt Leben, a German organization aimed at better independent living for people with disabilities (G); dpi.org /links.html—DPI, Disabled Peoples' International (E); sath.org—Society for Accessible Travel and Hospitality (U.S.) (E); gimponthego.com—Gimp on the Go, international accessibility for travelers with disabilities (E); movado.de—Movado, Tourism for All, see *Touring Berlin by Wheelchair* (E, G); bigub.de—Barrierefreies Internet (Barrier-Free Internet) (G); behinderteninfo.de—one of the best German sites for issues concerning the disabled (G)

Sex und Sitten (Sex and Morals)

Probably the single most important aspect that sets German and European social and sexual mores apart from those in the English-speaking world is the lack of any Puritan past. A glance through almost any mainstream German magazine, with its casual display of photos of naked or semi-naked women, graphically illustrates that point. Even some German newspapers have the standard page-two topless photo every day—a practice that would raise eyebrows in Iowa but doesn't cause so much as a nod in Niedersachsen.

Despite their casual attitude about nudity, Germans have never been counted among the world's great lovers. Casanova (1725–98) was Italian; Don Juan was a legendary Spaniard. Germans, rightly or wrongly, are not noted for being passionate paramours. Although Germans like to think of themselves as romantics, it is only in a dreamy, more intellectual sense. (*Die Romantik* was a German literary epoch around the beginning of the 19th century.) A German's idea of "romantic" is a trip to Italy.

Sex, however, is another matter. Almost any German town of average size has its designated red-light district, where regulated houses of prostitution can be found. This phenomenon is most apparent in Hamburg's notorious *Reeperbahn* "entertainment" district, or at nightfall in certain sections of Berlin's Mitte district, where throngs of streetwalkers (*Straßenstrich, Autostrich*) often cause minor traffic jams. Even smaller German towns often have a designated *Dirnenviertel* or *Rotlichtrevier* (red-light district) with so-called Eros-

Centers (formerly called *Bordelle* or *Freudenhäuser*), and *Callgirl* is now a German word. Under German as well as most other Western European law, prostitution, both heterosexual and homosexual, is for the most part not a punishable offense, and the trade is regulated for health reasons. In its refusal to close down a hooker (*Nutten*) operation associated with a Berlin bar, a German court also declared that prostitution was no longer considered *Sittenwidrig* (immoral, illegal). However, the Netherlands, not Germany, is the only European country that has actually fully legalized prostitution.

Yet, in spite of the court's claim and the efforts of Beate Uhse (1919–2001), Germany's most famous promoter of sexual liberation (and owner of a large chain of sex shops), the sex industry in general continues to be plagued by double standards, a sleazy image, and criminal elements—in Germany as elsewhere. Since the 1970s, prostitutes in France, Germany, the Netherlands, and a few other European countries have formed their own associations or unions. In Germany, a prostitute's income (*Dirnenlohn*) is legally subject to income taxes and a law that went into effect in 2002 made prostitutes eligible for health and retirement benefits.

Related Web links: beateuhse.de—Beate Uhse (adult content) (E, G); **fau.org**—a German prostitutes union site (G)

Gays and Lesbians in Germany: Pink Triangles and Paragraph 175

Widely considered the "father of the gay rights movement," the German physician Dr. Magnus Hirschfeld (1868–1935) founded the Scientific Humanitarian Committee (das Wissenschaftlich-humanitäre Komitee) in 1897. While urging public figures in Germany to openly support homosexual rights, Hirschfeld wrote that "the liberation of homosexuals can only be the work of homosexuals themselves." He believed homosexuality to be a natural, biological trait deserving scientific investigation rather than scorn. Hirschfeld, a *transvestite*, coined the term *transvestism* and published many volumes on the topic. He even played himself in the sex-information silent film *Different from the Others* (*Anders als die Anderen*) in 1919. That same year, he founded the Institute for Sexual Science in Berlin, which carried out research on "the third sex" and the causes of homosexuality. He brought the formerly taboo topic into public discussion and fought for the repeal of Germany's Paragraph 175, a law dating back to 1871 making sex between males a crime subject to imprisonment.

The rise of German fascism in the 1920s ushered in a much less enlightened attitude toward homosexuals. Hirschfeld, who was Jewish, was forced into exile in France in 1930, and his institute became a prime target of the book burning on Berlin's Opernplatz on May 10, 1933. While the Nazis forced Jews to wear yellow stars, homosexuals were put in concentration camps and wore pink triangles. The Nazis made Paragraph 175 even more strict, partly in reaction to Berlin's wide-open gay and lesbian scene (*Schwulen- und Lesbenszene*) in the 1920s and early '30s. It is therefore ironic that a prominent Nazi, Ernst Röhm, the head of the SA (*Sturmabteilung*—storm troopers), was a known homosexual. His elimination on Hitler's orders in 1934 was probably more for political reasons, but the National Socialists persecuted gays throughout their 12-year reign.

Although gays and lesbians in Germany now enjoy more tolerant attitudes and certain legal protections, Paragraph 175 was not completely abolished until 1994. The German political scene in recent years has produced some successful openly gay candidates at the local and state levels, although German gay and lesbian groups are still confronting conservative politicians over the issue of same-sex marriage. Most larger German cities, led by Berlin (which elected an openly gay mayor in 2001), have thriving, open gay communities. Even Munich's Oktoberfest features the *Bräurosl* "gay day," and the city's gay radio station is called Uferlos, which means "boundless." It is noteworthy that Catholic Bavaria was free of the repressive antigay laws found in Protestant Prussia in the late 19th century.

Related Web links: lsvd.de—LSVD online, Lesben- und Schwulenverband in Deutschland (Lesbian and Gay Association in Germany) (G); huk.org—Homosexuelle und Kirche (Homosexuals and the Church Ecumenical Group) (E, G); pink-triangle.org—Pink Triangle (E)

Die Beschäftigung mit dem Tode ist die Wurzel der Kultur. *("Dealing with death is the root of culture.")*

— FRIEDRICH DÜRRENMATT (1921–90), SWISS AUTHOR AND DRAMATIST

The German way of death is perhaps even more regulated than the German way of life. The German propensity to regulate almost every aspect of daily life carries over into the afterlife, with Germany's funeral industry among the most regulated in the world.

If, for instance, you want to spread Grandpa's ashes in the woods where he loved to hike, you'll find that it's verboten in some German *Länder* (states). The laws concerning cremation, *die Feuerbestattung*, are clear. Cremains must be in an appropriate container and placed in a cemetery or mausoleum. As a result of such heavy-handed restrictions, many urns in German cemeteries are missing or empty, their contents having been illegally placed elsewhere.

Critics of Germany's laws concerning funerals and cemeteries in the state of North Rhine-Westphalia (Nordrhein–Westfalen, NRW) point out that the strictures date back to 1934 and the Third Reich. While most of Germany's European neighbors long ago liberalized such laws, Germany's funeral industry (*das Bestattungsgewerbe*) has successfully prevented any relaxation of the regulation of funerals, burial, and cremation.

Even after you're legally and properly buried in a German cemetery, your resting place is only temporary. Because Germany is such a densely populated country and land is scarce, your right to "rest in peace" is limited to a certain term of years, usually 10 to 30, after which you're kicked out and your spot goes to some "body" else.

Related Web links: postmortal.de—Der Tod in Deutschland (Death in Germany), a site devoted to changing Germany's overregulated funeral industry (G); **begraebnis.at**—an Austrian funeral site with information about Austrian (Catholic) aspects of dealing with burials (G)

From Benz to Porsche

As Karl Benz drove his noisy, gasoline-powered, three-wheeled *Motorenwagen* through the streets of Mannheim in 1885, he could not have begun to imagine what an amazing impact his new invention would have on the world. About the same time, Gottlieb Daimler was working on a similar motorcar near Stuttgart. Although they lived only a few hundred miles apart, Daimler and Benz never met. The companies they each had formed were merged in 1926 to create the industrial giant known as Daimler-Benz AG until 1998. Seventy-two years after the first merger, a second created DaimlerChrysler AG by combining Daimler-Benz AG and America's Chrysler Motors.

Neither Benz nor Daimler would have had an internal combustion engine to run the first *Motorenwagen* had not Nikolaus August Otto invented the gasoline-powered engine in 1861. Otto went on to develop the four-stroke engine in (1878) and founded his own company to manufacture engines. Daimler and fellow engineer Wilhelm Maybach worked with Otto until they left to start their own company in 1882. Eight years later, Daimler founded the Daimler-Motoren-Gesellschaft, and around 1900, Maybach helped design the first Mercedes car, named for Daimler's daughter.

Germans still prefer to buy and drive the vehicles they are so good at manufacturing. Foreign automakers have a hard time in the German market, but German automakers such as Audi (VW), BMW, DaimlerChrysler, Opel (GM), Porsche, and Volkswagen are known worldwide.

The five Opel brothers began manufacturing bicycles in Rüsselsheim in 1886. Today the firm known as Adam Opel AG, now a division of General Motors, is one of Germany's largest automakers. Volkswagen is Europe's largest automaker and one of the world's best-known auto brands. Stuttgart is home to two famous car brands: Mercedes (DaimlerChrysler) and Porsche. The Bayrische Motorenwerke (BMW) calls Munich home.

Names Associated with the Automobile and Its Development

DEVELOPER	INVENTION/CONTRIBUTION
Karl Benz (1844–1929)	first practical automobile (1885)
Robert Bosch (1861–1942)	spark plug (1902); magneto
Gottlieb Daimler (1834–1900)	first motorcycle (1885); founded Daimler-Motoren-Gesellschaft (1890)
Rudolf Diesel (1858–1913)	diesel engine (1892)
Eugen Langen (1833–95)	worked with Nikolaus Otto; suspended monorail
Wilhelm Maybach (1864–1929)	design of the first Mercedes (1900–01)
Adam Opel (1837–95)	founded Adam Opel AG, now part of GM
Nikolaus Otto (1832–91)	first gasoline engine (1861); four-stroke version (1878)
Ferdinand Porsche (1875–1951)	design of the first Volkswagen (1934)

Related Web links: bmw.de—BMW (E, G);
bosch.de—Bosch AG (G); **volkswagen.de**—
Volkswagen AG (G); **daimlerchrysler.com**—
DaimlerChrysler (E)

Germans prefer to drive German-made cars.

Driving in Deutschland

The $2,000 driver's license is only the beginning! Germans are crazy about their cars and take driving seriously. How seriously? Well, a German driver's license (*Führerschein*) costs $1,500 to $2,000 and requires a minimum of 25 to 45 hours of professional instruction plus 12 hours of theory. (The largest share of the expense comes from the fees for mandatory driving lessons. Thus are German parents spared the joys of teaching their offspring to drive.) It does seem like a slightly better bargain once you realize that a German driver's license is good for life and never has to be renewed.

A non-German resident is allowed to drive for up to one year with a foreign license. If you are going to be living in Germany for more than one year, it is wise to begin the process of getting a German license after you have been in the country for six months, well in advance of the end of the one-year period. What you have to do to get your new *Führerschein* is largely a matter of geography, timing, luck, and money.

A foreign resident in Germany can usually acquire a German license for much less than a German starting out as a beginning driver—about $600 to $800. The cost comes in the form of paying for things like the following: an eye test (from a licensed optician, of course), a translation of your home license into German, fees (written exam, driving school lessons/test, certificates, and so forth), and the required first aid course.

If you are lucky, you will have a license from a country or one of the dozen or so U.S. states with which Germany has a reciprocity agreement. That can help you avoid some of the hoops through which less fortunate folks have to jump—although they are largely the same hoops a German citizen confronts. To get a license, Germans 18 years of age or older must attend a driving school (*Fahrschule*) and take both a written and a practical test. The practical exam is thorough and includes driving in a variety of situations—city streets, autobahn, and so forth.

Studying the German traffic rules for the written exam is a good idea even if you don't have to take the exam. Germany and Europe have some rules of the road that differ significantly from American practice. Probably the most important difference is the right-priority rule. Unless signs indicate otherwise, vehicles coming from the right have the right-of-way. Also, since most German road signs are symbols, without words (*ohne Worte*), it is wise to learn to recognize the many signs that may not be familiar to a foreigner.

Related Web link: germany-info.org—Germany Online–German Embassy–German Information Center—see *Search*, and key in "Driving in Germany" for information on converting a driver's license (E)

Flensburg and the KBA: Keeping Score on Germany's Drivers

The German city of Flensburg lies just a stein's throw from Denmark on the Flensburg Fjord. Situated almost as far north as one can go without leaving Germany, Flensburg is much more than just another place on the map for Germany's drivers, for it is in Flensburg that one finds the German institution known as the Kraftfahrt-Bundesamt (KBA), Germany's federal department of motor vehicles. Since 1974, the KBA has been responsible for keeping track of drivers' traffic violation points and maintaining a central registry for all of Germany.

When a driver is caught violating one of the provisions in Germany's Straßen-verkehrs-Ordnung (StVO, "traffic regulations"), the police notify the KBA. The KBA in turn records and archives the number of points for each violation. Any driver who accumulates a total of 18 points automatically loses his or her license. A single serious violation can earn a driver 7 points. Drunken driving (Trunkenheit am Steuer), leaving the scene of an accident (Verkehrsunfallflucht), and driving in the wrong direction on the autobahn (Fahren entgegen der Fahrtrichtung auf der Auto-bahn) are all rated at 7 points each. Minor violations will earn a driver 1 point. More serious offenses, however, have various point values up to the maximum of 7. Running a red light, for example, will draw 4 points.

The Flensburg point system is rigid. Drivers can't even contest any of their points until after the license has been revoked. They also can't dispute the KBA's records. Points for minor violations last for two years. Points for more serious offenses stay in the Flensburg registry for 10 years.

Motorists can request their Kontostand, or account balance, from Flensburg in writing. Germany's privacy laws prohibit phone or E-mail requests via the KBA's website. Until recently, a driver who had reached 14 points automatically received a so-called blauer Brief (blue letter) warning notification. A new law that took effect in 2000 warns drivers earlier and allows them to "work off" a limited number of points by attending a voluntary special driving class. A motorist with 8 points can get up to 4 of them deleted by sitting in the classroom, but drivers who have between 9 and 13 points can reduce their totals by only 2 points. Since the moving-violation points never expire, this is an important revision. Although a German driver's license is good for life, Germany's drivers aren't prone to be reckless. Of the country's 50 million drivers, only 17,000 (0.3 percent) have ever lost their licenses.

Related Web links: kba.de—Kraftfahrt-Bundesamt Flensburg (Federal Motor Transport Authority), see Index for the *Punkekatalog* listing of penalty points (E, G); **dvr.de**—Deutsche Verkehrssicherheitsrat (German Traffic Safety Organization) (G); **german-way.com/german/driving.html**—information on driving in Germany (E)

Public Transportation

Although Germans are known for their love of the automobile and driving, Germany is a place where one can generally get around easily without a car. All German cities of average or larger size have extensive, well-used public transportation systems consisting of a mix of buses, streetcars, and commuter rail lines. Berlin, Frankfurt am Main, Hamburg, Stuttgart, and Munich all have metro systems that run above and below ground. The German underground metros are referred as the U-Bahn, while the above-ground commuter rail lines are known as the S-Bahn. Soon you will learn that the U-Bahn sometimes runs above ground, while there are also subterranean S-Bahn lines.

S-Bahn stations are marked by a circular sign with a large green S. U-Bahn stations are indicated by a big blue U. Bus and tram stops are marked with a large H on a yellow circular sign. Both the S-Bahn and U-Bahn use an open-entry system without turnstyles or ticket collectors. As with buses and streetcars, you are required to purchase a ticket prior to boarding. You can save money by buying special all-day, weekly, monthly, student, senior, or multiple tickets (*Streifenkarten/Sammelkarten*, a strip of four to seven tickets). Unless you have a long-term pass, you must also cancel your ticket by using a red or yellow *Entwerter* that is located on the platform of the S-Bahn and U-Bahn or inside the bus or tram. You are not even supposed to be on the platform without a valid ticket, but under Germany's honor system, no one will check. However, occasional sting operations on the S-Bahn and U-Bahn catch and fine passengers who haven't been completely "honorable."

In Frankfurt and Munich, the S-Bahn also conveniently links downtown (*die City*) and the airport (*der Flughafen*). In Frankfurt, it takes a mere 12 minutes to make the trip. In Munich, you should allow about 45 minutes.

Related Web links: Public transportation authorities: **bvg.de**—BVG, Berlin (E, G); **hvv.de**— HVV, Hamburg (G); **vrr.de**—Verkehrsverbund Rhein-Ruhr, Düsseldorf/Dortmund region (G); **vvs.de**—VVS, Stuttgart (G); **mvv-muenchen.de**—MVV, Munich (G); **vrsinfo.de**— Verkehrsverbund Rhein-Sieg, Cologne/Bonn region (G); **rmv.de**—Rhein-Main Verkehrsverbund, Frankfurt region (G); **vrn.de**—Verkehrsverbund Rhein-Neckar, Mannheim region (G); **vbn.de**— Verkehrsverbund Bremen/Niedersachsen, Bremen region (G); **evag.de**—EVAG, Essen (G)

Riding the German Rails

Traveling by train in Europe can be a lot more pleasant if you know a few tricks of the trade. Because all large to medium-size cities, as well as many smaller communities, in German-speaking Europe have a train station (or two or three), train travel is convenient and efficient, although increasingly expensive. The main train station (*Hauptbahnhof*) is usually in the center of town, from which commuter trains, taxis, streetcars, and buses can take the traveler straight to a local destination. The weakest link in this otherwise efficient chain is often the Deutsche Bahn ticket office at the station, where it seems there are always too few ticket agents. Long lines and long waits are all too common. (Tip: Use DB's website to purchase tickets online.)

Although the privatized Deutsche Bahn AG finally entered the modern financial era in 1992 by accepting credit cards, bearers of plastic must still be wary. Look for logos and/or a sign (sometimes handwritten) that mentions *Kreditkarten* or "credit cards." You can't just walk up to any ticket window and expect to use your card, even though that is common practice in much of the world. Also, don't assume you'll be able to use a credit card to purchase train tickets at every one of the more than 5,000 rail stations in Germany, although it has become more common. You should even ask in advance at a German travel agency to be sure it accepts credit card payment for rail tickets. German Rail's BahnCard used to also function as a Visa card, but it is now only a discount card that you may want to consider using.

It can cut the cost of a train ticket in half and is worth buying if you will be traveling frequently by rail.

European trains are divided into first and second class. Look for a large "1" or "2" painted on the car near the door. In general, first-class rail travel costs about double the second-class rate. Some special trains (EC, IC, ICE, and so forth) also have a surcharge, or *Zuschlag*, added to the price of the ticket. If you have not already paid the surcharge, the conductor will require payment (in cash) when checking your ticket. The surcharge for high-speed ICE trains varies, depending on the connection.

You can use the practical *Wagenstand-anzeiger* (car locator) to find your train car on the long rail platform and avoid walking through half the train to find your seat. The platform is divided into sections labeled "A" to "E." The car locator can tell you almost to the nearest meter where your car will stop.

Related Web links: **bahn.de**—Deutsche Bahn AG, a good site that also offers online ticket purchasing (E, G); **reiseauskunft.bahn.de**—Deutsche Bahn's online rail ticket and schedule information (E, G); **eurail.com**—Eurail (E); **dbmuseum.de**—Deutsche Bahn Museum—this rail transportation museum is located in Nuremberg (E, G); **sbb.ch**—SBB Online, Swiss railroad (E, G); **oebb.at**—ÖBB, Austrian railway (G); **rail-info.ch**—various private rail lines in Switzerland (E, G)

Der Liegewagen Versus the ICE

Some rail travel enthusiasts have come to appreciate *couchette* travel, while others use it only as a last resort or never. Offered by most European railways, a *couchette* car (*Liegewagen*) features compartments that have regular seats by day and sleeping bunks by night. Such *Nachtzüge* (night trains) are usually scheduled to leave in the late afternoon and arrive in the morning. (More expensive Pullman/*Schlafwagen* accommodations are also available on *Nachtzüge*.) Intended for longer overnight journeys such as Berlin–Paris or Hamburg–Munich, the *couchette* seats on each side of the compartment magically transform into four or six bunks. The porter drops off a blanket, a pillow, and a pocket-like sheet for each person. After some clever unfolding and the snapping of a few latches, the bunks are ready. There is no real privacy, and you probably won't know most of the people in the compartment. Your traveling companions may be male or female, young or old, and from any part of the world. *Couchette* travel is not for timid souls. It can be a fascinating adventure, a sleepless night, or both. You must make reservations for a *Liegewagen*, and there is a per-person *couchette* surcharge of 13.40 euros for six beds or 20 euros for four beds.

The increasing use of high-speed trains such as the German ICE (InterCityExpress) and the French TGV has reduced the need for overnight *couchette* travel in Germany and Europe. Deutsche Bahn (then still the old Bundesbahn) put its first ICE trains into service in 1991. Since then, several newer generations of the ICE have evolved. Today's German ICE can whisk you between Hamburg in the north and Munich in the south in less than six hours. In the old days, not so many years ago, the same trip took more than eight hours.

The sleekly styled ICE 3 that began service in 2000 can reach a top speed of 330 kilometers (205 miles) per hour and, like all other ICEs, offers a quiet, jetliner-like interior (but roomier than a jet) with chair-back video screens, audio headsets, fax machines, and telephones. Because of their high speed, ICE cars are pressurized as well as air-conditioned. The ICE T is a "leaning" train that runs faster on regular lines not designed for the standard ICEs. The Dutch and Spanish railways have purchased versions of the German ICE for use in their countries.

Related Web links: bahn.de—Deutsche Bahn AG, search "CityNightLine" or "Nachtzug" (E, G); http://mercurio.iet.unipi.it/ice/ice.html—ICE, European rail server with lots of interesting information about German rail travel, from Tobias Köhler's unofficial rail site, including ICE photos and floor plans (E, G)

Europe—especially Germany and France—has seen an increase in the use of high-speed trains.

Schwarzfahrer: Don't Forget That Ticket!

Germany's extensive public transportation network functions for the most part on an honor system. Unlike subway or metro systems in most other countries, the commuter rail system in large and medium-size German cities and in Vienna has no tollgates or other barriers in S-Bahn (urban commuter line) or U-Bahn (underground/subway) stations. Since there are also no conductors on these conveyances, passengers are expected to have a valid ticket or pass in their possession before boarding a streetcar, train, or bus.

On average, fewer than 4 percent of Germany's daily commuters try to travel without a valid ticket. However, in certain areas and certain stations, the rate can be as high as 10 percent. In a recent crackdown over a period of six months by Hamburg's HVV public transportation authority, 150,000 fare dodgers (*Schwarzfahrer*) had to pay a 40 euro ($38) fine for not having a ticket. That was 3.6 percent of the total 4.2 million passengers that HVV checked. Current fines for traveling on public transport without a ticket range from 30 to 40 euros in most German cities. This is a bargain compared to 62 euros in Paris.

Following its expansion after reunification, Berlin's metro system (BVG) has considered introducing a tollgate system with magnetic-striped tickets similar to that found in London, New York, and Paris. The hitch is that installing such a system in every S-Bahn or U-Bahn station would be an expensive way to combat increasing numbers of *Schwarzfahrer* in the German capital.

Although in most German-speaking cities, you can buy a ticket from bus or streetcar drivers, it is cheaper to buy a *Sammelkarte* or *Streifenkarte*, offering several tickets together at a discount. There are usually also special tickets or passes for the day, week, or month, as well as discounted student and senior tickets. At many locations, you will find automatic ticket machines (*Fahrkartenautomaten*). Larger stations generally have a ticket booth where you can purchase any kind of ticket. Once you have a ticket, it is good on all buses, streetcars, and S-Bahn and U-Bahn trains within a city's network. Just don't forget to validate your ticket in the *Entwerter* or *Entgelter* located either at stations or inside buses and streetcars. An unstamped ticket is the same as no ticket.

Related Web links: bahn.de—Deutsche Bahn AG, German rail (E, G); **bvg.de**—Berlin's public transportation authority (E, G); **hvv.de**—Hamburg's public transportation authority (G)

Automatic ticket machines are found at many locations.

BahnCard or Eurailpass?

One big advantage of having a Eurailpass, Flexipass, Europass, or German Rail Pass, besides any cost savings, is that you can avoid ticket-buying hassles. You'll have to confront a Deutsche Bahn (DB) ticket window only to make reservations, if you want them— advisable during peak travel periods in the summer or on popular trains. These special passes have to be purchased in advance and may have restrictions. A Eurailpass, for example, may be obtained only in non-European countries. Germany, Austria, and Switzerland each have their own rail pass offers. (See a travel agent or the DB website if you want details.)

The BahnCard is another good idea, if you will be using the train regularly over a period of time in Germany. It won't spare you the task of buying train tickets, but the BahnCard will give you a 50 percent reduction in the cost of any tickets you buy during a one-year period (13 months with a subscription). You can decide the first day the BahnCard will become valid. The second-class BahnCard costs 140 euros. A "Senior" (for people age 60 or over) or a "Junior" (for ages 18 to 22) BahnCard is only 70 euros. The so-called BahnCard First (the first-class version) will set you back 280 euros. (See the DB website for current prices.) Special lower-cost versions of the BahnCard are available for students, teens, married couples, young children, and families. The card is not valid for special reduced-priced tickets, and any supplementary charges have to be paid in full. But the BahnCard is valid on every day of the year, including holidays. The card is issued to you in your name like a credit card but, again, is not a credit card.

When you're walking through a car of your train looking for a seat without having a reservation, notice the orange reservation ("*Reserviert*") cards slipped into holders on the luggage racks above the seats. If you have a reservation, you're looking for your own card above your designated seat(s). If you don't have a reservation, you are looking for the cards so you can avoid sitting in a reserved seat. The card will tell you which segment of the train's route has been reserved for that seat. If you are getting off before the reserved segment, then you can sit there without worry. If you happen to be sitting in a reserved seat, the person entitled to that seat will ask you to relinquish it. The conductor who comes by to check tickets will verify the seat reservation if there is one.

Related Web links: bahn.de—Deutsche Bahn AG, a good site that also offers online ticket purchasing (E, G); reiseauskunft.bahn.de— Deutsche Bahn's online rail ticket and schedule information (E, G); eurail.com—Eurail (E)

Quizlink Answers

Do as the Germans Do
1. a, 2. c, 3. abc (trick question—all three), 4. c, 5. b, 6. c, 7. a, 8. a, 9. c, 10. b, 11. b, 12. b, 13. c, 14. b

Places
1. (a) i, (b) iii, (c) ii; 2. a; 3. c; 4. none (trick question); 5. b; 6. a

People
1. b, 2. c, 3. a, 4. a, 5. b, 6. b, 7. c, 8. b, 9. a, 10. c, 11. b, 12. b

Organizations
1. a, 2. a, 3. b, 4. c, 5. a, 6. b, 7. c, 8. c, 9. b

Time
1. c, 2. b, 3. b, 4. a, 5. c, 6. b, 7. a, 8. b, 9. b, 10. c

Quantity
1. c, 2. a, 3. c, 4. c, 5. b, 6. c, 7. b

Connections
1. b, 2. c, 3. b, 4. a, 5. c, 6. c, 7. a, 8. c, 9. c, 10. a

What's That?
1. a, 2. c, 3. a, 4. a, 5. a

Laws and Regulations
1. c, 2. c, 3. b, 4. a, 5. c, 6. a, 7. b, 8. c, 9. c, 10. b

Know What the Germans Know
1. c, 2. b, 3. c, 4. b, 5. a, 6. b, 7. a, 8. c, 9. c, 10. b, 11. c, 12. c

Index

INDEX

INDEX